# WORK MATTERS

# WORK MATTERS

*How Parents' Jobs Shape*
*Children's Well-Being*

## MAUREEN PERRY-JENKINS

PRINCETON UNIVERSITY PRESS

PRINCETON AND OXFORD

Published by Princeton University Press
41 William Street, Princeton, New Jersey 08540
99 Banbury Road, Oxford OX2 6JX

press.princeton.edu

All Rights Reserved
ISBN 9780691174693
ISBN (e-book) 9780691185866

British Library Cataloging-in-Publication Data is available

Editorial: Meagan Levinson and Jacqueline Delaney
Production Editorial: Sara Lerner
Text Design: Karl Spurzem
Production: Erin Suydam
Publicity: James Schneider and Kathryn Stevens
Copyeditor: Kathleen Kageff

Jacket photo and design by Amanda Weiss

This book has been composed in Arno Pro and Outfit

Printed on acid-free paper. ∞

Printed in the United States of America

10 9 8 7 6 5 4 3 2 1

# CONTENTS

# PREFACE

The idea for this study first emerged during an interview with a thirty-two-year-old mother, whom I will call Jodie, who worked in a food packing plant.[1] As a newly minted assistant professor at the University of Illinois, I set out to study the experiences of working-class parents who were raising school-aged children. Jodie, one of the participants in my initial study, had just come home from her job at the nearby food plant, and I was asking her about the challenges facing her and her husband. They were managing split shifts at work while dealing with the busy schedules of their two children, who played sports, attended church activities twice a week, and needed help with their endless amounts of homework. As she described her typical day, she suddenly stopped and said, "You know, compared to when my kids were little, this is nothing. This is a piece of cake. Going back to work after a few weeks and leaving my new baby with someone else. Now that was hell." She then looked at me and said, "That is really the study you should be doing."

I pondered Jodie's words all the way home. I knew there was an enormous literature on the initial transition to parenthood, but what did we know about the transition back to work after having a baby? I soon discovered that we didn't know much, and what we did know focused primarily on White, middle-class, two-parent families. The limited research indicated that, despite having far more resources than low-income families to

manage this second transition, these families still found returning to work to be incredibly difficult. How, then, did low-
income families cope with work while becoming new parents,
and how did that process affect their own and their children's
well-being?

The study described in this book was an attempt to answer
those questions. Specifically, it was an attempt to examine how
the transition to parenthood, coupled with the second transition
back to paid employment soon after birth, affected new parents'
mental health, their ability to parent, and, ultimately, their children's development. The research you will read about was twenty
years in the making and made possible by the commitment of
twenty graduate students and literally hundreds of undergradu-
ates. Our work has generated numerous scholarly articles, but
in contrast to these prior publications, which focus primarily on
the information from parent and child questionnaires, the aim
of my book is to look behind the numbers to tell the deeply personal stories of new mothers and fathers trying to be good workers, good partners, and good parents in the face of immense
challenges. The parents in this study allowed us to audiotape
their answers to myriad questions about their struggles and successes, as well as videotape interactive activities between them
and their children. Many agreed to participate because they
wanted to make a difference for others. They hoped that their
stories could highlight the challenges faced by low-income families and point to places where changes in workplace, state, and
federal policies could support families raising the next generation. These parents are the heroes of this book.

As my team and I followed these families through one of the
most momentous and meaningful events in their lives—
becoming a parent—we were humbled and awed by their ability to rise above the business and disruptions of daily life to

create meaningful lives. Depending on when we walked into their lives, we witnessed very different scenarios. Sometimes we found them coping well with their newborn but facing tremendous obstacles as they transitioned back to work. At other times, work served as an escape, or at least a reprieve, from caring for a difficult child. One fact became crystal clear over the course of this project: there is no one story reflecting a monolithic experience for low-wage, working parents and their children. Instead, there are many different stories, which together reveal the varied ways that families and workplaces interact, morph, conflict, and cooperate to shape lives.

Despite the vast range of family experiences you will read about in this book, there were also some consistent themes that emerged. For example, almost all families were coping with the stress of securing and maintaining affordable, quality child care. Most had short, unpaid parental leaves and had to return to their paid jobs far sooner than they wanted. Yet, nearly all expressed having a new sense of purpose in life, feeling a deep sense of responsibility for this new child, and also feeling new hope and excitement.

All the stories shared in this book provide lessons about how to cope effectively during this stressful transition; more importantly, they provide lessons about the ways in which workplace policies and conditions could be changed to support new parents and the healthy development of their children. Finally, I hope these stories challenge us all to rethink our values regarding the attention and care we give to both parents and children in our society, and recognize that under the right conditions, parents do not have to feel torn between work and family, but rather enriched by both.

As I was finishing this book, the world was hit with a pandemic the likes of which had not been seen for nearly a century.

The financial hardships brought on by Covid-19 have fallen most heavily on low-income workers, who are the least able to withstand the financial shock. Many of the families who participated in this project are suffering. Those I talked with during the early months of the pandemic were receiving unemployment and limping along, but many were concerned that their benefits would expire before they were able to return to work. In these circumstances, the dire need to have a job eclipsed any discussion of job satisfaction or supports. In a challenging economy, our efforts to improve workplace policies and conditions often come to a swift halt, and we return to the most basic need—bringing in a paycheck. However, we must not be short-sighted. We need to remember that the next generation, who are children now, are being shaped by the financial and work challenges facing families at this very moment. What we do to support low-wage workers, hit the hardest by this event, will be critical for the health and well-being of working parents and their children.

# ACKNOWLEDGMENTS

In our world today, as we are facing significant global challenges such as climate change, wars, pandemics, systemic racism, and gun violence, it is amazing that people continue to engage in one of the most life-changing and hopeful acts I can think of . . . having a baby. Yet the majority of adults continue to do so. This story is about the life-changing and irrational act of becoming a parent, while holding down a full-time, low-wage job; and it is the story of how this event shapes the health and well-being of parents and their children. I am indebted to all the families who participated in this project, who took hours out of their busy lives to share their journeys. I learned much about fortitude, gratefulness, and love. I thank you all for your honesty and openness—your stories have much to teach us.

I gratefully acknowledge the ten years of research support for this project provided by the National Institute of Mental Health (grants R29-MH56777 and R01-MH56777). The first grant was in response to a call for proposals for research focused on the role of social context and disparities in shaping the lives of families. This important vision at NIMH at the time, a vision that acknowledged not only the impact of social context but the value of studying developmental change over time, made this work possible.

I have had the joy of working with the most dedicated, creative, and smart graduate students on the planet. My warmest thanks go to this team of phenomenal individuals: Abbie Goldberg, Courtney Pierce, Heather-Lyn Haley, Bill Miller, Heather Bourne, Holly Laws, JuliAnna Smith, Bilal Ghandour, Kelly Graceffa, Karen Meteyer, Amy Claxton, Jade Logan, Betsy Turner, Aya Ghunney, Katie Newkirk, Hillary Paul Halpern, Rachel Herman, Andrea Craft, Christina Rowley, and Diego Barcala-Delgado. I am also indebted to my friend and colleague Mary D'Alessandro, who managed the Work and Family Transitions Project for years. She truly was the "heart" of our team, running the show with skill, clarity of purpose, and commitment.

We collected data from 360 families, conducted four in-home interviews and one mail survey per family, and for some conducted follow-up interviews years later. Based on my calculations, this amounted to about fifteen hundred interviews. We spent countless hours driving around western Massachusetts, in all types of weather, and engaged in long, emotional, and sometimes difficult conversations with parents. We primarily worked nights and weekends because that's when parents were home. This was not your typical research assistantship, and the students that signed up to work with me were anything but "typical." I thank all of them, from the bottom of my heart, for understanding the importance of our work, for their invaluable contributions to the scholarship, and for going above and beyond the call of duty. They are amazing scholars and even better human beings.

This book was years in the making, and I am indebted to so many who were mentors, colleagues, and friends on the journey.

As I started graduate school, I was lucky enough to be assigned to Nan Crouter as my mentor. I followed as she taught me the art and the science of conducting family research in the field, while modeling how to maintain a life at the same time. Over the years, her unflagging support carried me through the stressful pretenure years and the later years of building a career. Throughout it all she was my touchstone, always there to help solve a research problem, provide career advice, or share stories about our families. She was the perfect mentor, who became a dear friend, and I am grateful to have her in my life.

I am also thankful to Susan McHale, the other half of the "Nan and Susan" team, who modeled for all their graduate students the fine art of collaboration and friendship. And to my graduate school "siblings"—Shelley MacDermid Wadsworth, Aaron Ebata, Brenda Volling, Anisa Zvonkovic, Terri Cooney, Tamra Lair, Todd Bartko, Jim Mikesell, and Diana Mutchler—you all made the ride so much more fun. Finally, surviving during those early "assistant professor" years was only made possible with the love and support of my dear friends, Aaron Ebata and Laurie Kramer.

I owe a debt of gratitude to Dr. Joyce Everett, professor emerita at Smith College, who was a co-investigator on the second grant and who opened the eyes of our team in thinking about how racism and trauma shape the lives of new parents and their children. Her thoughtfulness and insight enriched all that we did.

Spending twenty-six years working with the colleagues in my department has been a gift. Their friendship has made me grateful to walk into work every day, even when it's been stressful—a rare find in academia. Special thanks to David Arnold, Kirby Deater-Deckard, Hal Grotevant, and Buju Dasgupta for years of good conversations and friendship. To Fran Deutsch, thank you for our hours-long conversations at Esselon, they always stimulated exciting new ideas. Finally, the Center for Research on Families at UMass stands out as my true academic home. It is a place that fosters interdisciplinary thinking, big ideas, and inclusiveness. My undying gratitude goes to Gisele, Wendy,

Amanda, Carla, Stepanie, Aline, and Holly, who helped to create the "magic" of CRF, where family scholars come to develop new projects, learn, and grow—all with good food and friendship. It is the place I have always felt the most "at home" to do my work, to challenge myself, and to thrive.

The impetus for this book came on a weekend getaway with three of my dearest friends and colleagues from UMass Amherst—Naomi Gerstel, Lisa Harvey, and Sally Powers. I will never forget the conversation. We were sitting around on a lazy Sunday morning, and I started to share a story about one of the families in my study. Someone asked me why these stories were never featured in my publications, which up to that point had all been quantitative papers. At that point Naomi adamantly pronounced, "You need to write a book." The conversation continued, and by the end of the weekend I had started an application for a fellowship for my upcoming sabbatical, and I was on my way toward writing a book . . . little did I know what that meant. They all spent hours reading my first, very long draft of this book, and filled it and subsequent drafts with comments, edits, and encouragement. I feel so lucky to have these wonderful women as my "work family." They are always ready for a good meal, a road trip, and an adventure, and I am deeply grateful for their friendship and support.

I was lucky enough to receive a fellowship to the Center for Advanced Study in Behavioral Sciences at Stanford University in 2015–16 with the aim of writing a book. My year at CASBS was life changing, and I am indebted to Margaret Levi for the opportunity. One of the first things I learned, however, was that I had no idea how to write a book. I will be forever grateful to Josh Gamson, who supportively, and as kindly as possible, let me know that the proposal I had submitted for the fellowship was far from a book proposal. He shared models, read drafts, and helped me inch along to a true book proposal. Natasha Iskander was a true friend that year, reading, listening, supporting, and, in her gentle way, pushing me to "just get it down on paper." Louis and Kate, a daring duo, were always there with words of wisdom and a good laugh. Finally, thank you to my CASBS writing group, Mick Smyer, Barbara Risman, Glenn Loury, Victoria Bernal, Joshua Gamson, and Natasha Iskander, who provided laughs, insights, and accountability.

I also met my editor Meagan Levinson for the first time at CASBS, and I knew immediately that I wanted her to shepherd this book through. She saw the value in the stories, was committed to the message, and was willing to hold this first-time book writer's hand through many versions. I thank her for her vision, her patience, and her enthusiasm; her insights and feedback have helped me to find the essence of the story.

Many friends, old and new, have been hearing about this book for a very long time. They cautiously ask, "How's the book coming?" not sure if my response will be some long-winded update or a short rebuff. But they've hung in there.

To my book club of over twenty years—Mary D'Alessandro Laura Drake, Jeanne Horrigan, Kelly Keane, Cathy Lawlor, Claire Norton, Betsy Cannon Smith, and Mary Ellen Sailer—I thank you for reading a very long, much too wordy version of this book and for still showering me with praise and support. Your ideas and suggestions made this book better. We lost one of our members this past year—our dear Mary Ellen. As she was fighting off the side effects of her chemo treatments, she would always rally to discuss the latest chapter or revision with me. She is in these pages, and I miss her deeply.

I am lucky enough to have a group of tried and true friends that have been with me since childhood. We have shared most of life's transitions, and all of us have struggled with parenthood, work, and partnerships over the years, the theme of this book. I have learned that support from friends is truly one of the most important things that gets you through. So, Audrey Long O'Connor, Alicia Testa Caritano, Susan White Murley, Laura Guay, Jeannie Maguire Robinson, Eileen Conway Rounds, and Peter Murley . . . thank you for sharing the past fifty years (and to your partners Neil, Mike, Don, and Rex, who put up with us). A special thank-you to Susan and Peter for providing my writing lair during the long pandemic, a place to write, think, and contemplate—it was true gift.

Finally, to my family: I grew up in a working-class home with four brothers and my parents, Mary and Cliff Perry. I watched work and family dynamics play out along strict, traditional gender lines, but I also saw parents working hard to create a good life for their children. As a child, I did not understand the financial stress they were under; in many ways I was protected from that burden; but I have come to understand how heavy that load must have been for them. My mother worked part-time as a waitress when we were young, usually at night so she could care for us during the day. My father was trained in electronics and became an electronics teacher at a vocational school early in my childhood, a job that, back then, you could do without a college degree. The buffer for me was that I was well loved.

To my four brothers, Bob, Rick Bud, and Scott, I feel lucky that I grew up in your midst. I learned much about love and kindness, fighting, negotiating, and compromise while living with you all. I also suspect my deep-seated interest in gender and power emerged from this early training.

My love and heartfelt thanks go to my three children, Christopher, Scott, and Emily. I have learned so much from each of you. You welcomed my many graduate and undergraduate students into our lives over the years, helped to host numerous parties, and listened to far too many interview stories over family dinners. You taught me why sane adults continue to engage in the irrational but amazing experience of becoming parents. As you have grown and included wonderful new partners into our family, Kara Himes, Mary Zhang, and Zach Friedlander, it is a joy to watch how you manage the challenges and successes of your own work and family acts. And to our wonderful Charlotte, our spunky, adorable, and amazing granddaughter . . . thank you for constantly teaching me to be present, have fun, and make sure there are always surprises.

Finally, to Michael, my partner in every way possible, I dedicate this book to you. We grew up as working-class kids who met in high school and are working on thirty-nine years of marriage. We had our first child, Christopher, in graduate school, and two others, Scott and Emily, as I was an assistant professor and Mike was a new managing engineer. We tried to do it all, and during those early years we were often exhausted and stretched thin. But we muddled through raising kids, holding down jobs, and maintaining our relationship . . . it was hard even though we had far more resources at our disposal than the families in this study have had—a lesson not lost on either of us.

Michael watched this book in the making, preparing dinners, running carpools, and supervising homework while I was out on interviews. He listened patiently, adding his insights and reactions, when I came home all pumped up after an interview. He traveled across the country multiple times and held down the fort at home as I followed my dream to write this book. He truly makes nothing seem impossible.

Michael, I thank you for your endless optimism and big dreams. What a lovely, messy, and exhilarating ride we have had together—I love you.

# WORK MATTERS

# CHAPTER 1

# "They Sure Don't Make It Easy for Parents"

*Low-Income, Working Parents and Their Children*

I first met Maria in September 2009. The young woman who greeted me at the door that day was obviously pregnant and, with her long black hair, glowing skin, and Beyonce t-shirt, looked all of sixteen years old. I knew from our phone screening, however, that Maria was twenty-one and in her third trimester of pregnancy. As I walked into the kitchen, the smell of breakfast and the murmurings of comfortable conversation filled the air. Gathered around a large Formica kitchen table, four adults, drinking coffee, and two toddlers were talking and sharing eggs, refried beans, and toast. The room fell silent as I entered. Maria quickly told them that I was from the university and there to learn about her pregnancy and plans for work. They smiled, offered me some coffee, and resumed their conversation. Maria gestured for me to join her in the living room, where it was quieter. This interview had originally been planned to happen with both Maria and Carlos, the baby's father, but the day before, Maria let me know Carlos couldn't join us because he had taken extra hours at the local supermarket, where he worked the deli counter.

Maria worked about thirty-five hours per week, making $8.50 an hour, in her job as a "Subway Sandwich Artist," a title whose irony wasn't lost on her. "Yup, that's my official job title—I make subs for people, and they call me an artist . . . really?" Maria had been on the job for only three months, and she was not yet sure how she felt about it. She enjoyed talking with customers, but she lamented that "it gets boring pretty fast." In addition to his job at the deli, her boyfriend, Carlos, was taking classes at the technical college in town with the goal of becoming an IT specialist. Between them, they cleared about $1,400 a month.

As Maria and I settled in for our first interview, I reiterated the main goal of the project—to learn how new parents juggle the demands of full-time work and caring for a baby—and reminded her that I would be interviewing her five times over the next year, so I could hear her story as it unfolded. After some small talk about how she had been feeling of late, I started by asking Maria a simple but loaded question: "How did you come to be an expectant mother at this point in your life?" Maria was not shy; she immediately shared that the pregnancy had been a surprise to her and her boyfriend. They had been dating for only eight months when she found out she was pregnant. She lived at home with her mother, her older sister, her sister's boyfriend, and her sister's two children. Carlos lived across town with his parents. As Maria noted, "We don't really know what we are doing at this point. The baby is due in four weeks, and the time is just flying by. In the beginning we both said we wanted to stay together because, you know, it's important for the baby to have two parents . . . but he sure isn't acting like that now." Maria was waiting for Carlos to "step up to the plate," in her words, and help plan for the upcoming year, but it wasn't happening.

I asked Maria if she had thought about how much time she planned to take off when the baby arrived. She told me that she hadn't talked with her boss about taking parental leave, nor had she really thought about how much time she would take off. "I am not sure what the rules are at work. I think I get some time off, maybe six weeks, but I am really not sure." She laughed. "Guess I should figure that out, huh?" I then asked her if she had any plans for who would care for the baby when she was back at work, "Not yet, I kind of just want to get through the birth, you know. I don't want to jump the gun; I want to have a healthy baby first."

With almost all the families we interviewed, stress about finances was an ever-present worry, and Maria was no exception. "I am always worried about money. I don't make a lot, and I pay my mom $250 a month for rent. Carlos and I talked about getting our own place but . . . then there is food, car payments, and clothes . . . my phone, gas for the car . . . whatever. I guess I am not good with money." When I asked her about the new expenses a baby would bring, she told me that her sister was giving her hand-me-downs, including a crib, clothes, and a high chair. "So, I am all set with that stuff." She then went on to raise the issue of child care. "I am thinking maybe Carlos can watch the baby when I am at work; maybe we can set up different schedules. Who knows if that will work? My neighbor has a family day care. I might try that, but she charges $2.50 an hour." Maria seemed troubled as she spoke about how she was going to find infant care that she could afford.

Hours later, after Maria had dutifully finished answering my questions and filling out all the survey questionnaires, we said our good-byes. I let her know I would be calling around the due date to see how things were going and to schedule our second interview. I thanked her for taking the time to share her story. She held up her hand and said, "No, no, I think I should thank you. All these questions have got me thinking about what I am heading into here. This is going to be . . . big, isn't it? So many decisions to make . . . kind of scary, but exciting. Time to get ready."[1]

## Becoming a Parent

Maria and Carlos's story, along with the stories of many other mothers and fathers who are having a baby and attempting to hold down full-time, low-wage jobs, are often invisible. We tend to hear, instead, about professional couples coping with the wage penalties associated with new motherhood, or women whose careers are derailed by the "mommy track" or an unequal division of housework.[2][3][4] When it comes to less affluent families, however, Americans most often hear about poor mothers, often single, scraping by with government support and unstable work. How low-income, employed mothers and fathers manage the demands of full-time work and new parenthood is a story we know much less about, despite the fact that this group makes up the largest portion of working parents in the country.[5] The challenges that low-income parents face are not adequately represented by middle-class narratives because low-wage workers deal with work conditions and policies that differ sharply from those of their more affluent counterparts. Nor are their stories captured in the narratives of the poor, who are often in and out of the labor force for much longer periods. This book brings the unique stories of low-income, working families to light, describes what is and is not working for them, and demonstrates that aspects of parents' work—both mothers' and fathers'—directly contribute to or detract from the healthy development of their children.

The transition to parenthood is an incredibly destabilizing life event for most people. Roles and responsibilities are in flux, priorities shift, and life must be managed with less sleep and structure. Low-income workers, in particular, often face tremendous stress during this sensitive period. They must manage the pressures of work and parenting with low wages, unpredictable and often insufficient work hours, last-minute scheduling, and few family-friendly benefits—all factors that can adversely affect their well-being and inhibit their ability to be engaged and sensitive parents.

The transition to parenthood can be particularly daunting for workers in the United States, one of the most inhospitable countries in the world to have a child, especially for low-wage parents. The United States not only offers one of the shortest parental leaves in the world but is also one of the few countries, along with New Guinea, Suriname, and a few South Pacific island nations, that do not offer paid parental leave (although this is starting to change at the state level).[6] Consequently, low-income parents, who often have few financial reserves, have little choice but to return to work very soon after their child's birth. Among the families in this study, even those eligible for unpaid leave could rarely afford to use the full twelve weeks offered through the federal Family and Medical Leave Act (FMLA). In addition, nearly every parent we talked to told us that twelve weeks did not feel like enough time to recover from childbirth, establish sleep and feeding routines, and set up child care before returning to work.

The resistance in the United States to adopting policies to support low-income, working families endangers the health and well-being of millions of children in this country during their first year of life, a critical time in human development. To put this point in perspective, it is estimated that during the first few years of life, more than one million neural connections form every second in the brain of a child.[7] Sensitive and responsible care from parents and other caregivers is the single most important ingredient for supporting this dramatic surge in brain development. Researchers at the Center for the Developing Child at Harvard University refer to these early years as the "bricks and mortar of brain development";[8] the basic foundation laid during this time determines the architecture for all subsequent development. If new parents are faced with overwhelming financial, relational, and personal problems during the first few years of parenthood and, as a result, are less able to provide attentive and responsive caregiving, a child's foundation becomes fragile. It is not overly dramatic or sensational to acknowledge that the current state of affairs for low-income families poses a serious risk to the well-being of our society.

The conditions just summarized, as well as conventional wisdom, might lead one to believe that Maria and Carlos's story will be just another sad tale of young parents struggling to hold down their jobs and raise a child. Rarely do we hear of low-income, working families functioning well. Yet, as we will see, their story, like those of many in this book, demonstrates the resilience that makes it possible for low-income families to thrive. In this book, I challenge the popular and monolithic image of struggling, unhappy, and depleted parents toiling away in unfulfilling and low-wage jobs. Indeed, many of the families we came to know maintained stable relationships, reported high levels of well-being, and raised children with positive social and cognitive outcomes. And yes, there were others who struggled mightily. They languished in stressful and unfulfilling jobs or moved from one job to another, experienced high levels of stress and depression, and often had children who lagged behind in social and cognitive skills. The question of why some low-income, working families do well across the early years of parenthood while others so often struggle is central to this book, and one that will be answered, in part, by focusing on the role of work.

## Understanding the Problem

What about parents' work matters for child development? How do work hours, wages, schedules, and policies relate to working mothers' and fathers' stress and well-being and, in turn, to the well-being of their children? And beyond these more structural aspects of work, how do job conditions—such as relationships with supervisors and coworkers, time pressure, or autonomy on the job—shape the lives of working parents, their ability to be warm and responsive parents, and, ultimately, their children's development?

I have spent most of my career studying these issues and, over the last twenty years, working with my students, have followed the lives of hundreds of low-income, working families about to have a child. We have had front-row seats to the momentous event of becoming a new parent. We saw severely sleep-deprived parents learn to change diapers, nurse, give baths, and love their new little humans. We also watched as they headed back to work, often weeks after birth, some depleted, some resigned, and almost all conflicted about how to be a good parent and worker. Throughout these years, we talked with them at their kitchen tables and on their back porches about their experiences.

The approach taken by this study charts new territory in a number of important ways. First, this project focuses explicitly on the work and family issues of low-income families, with no attempt to compare them to their more affluent counterparts. Much of the public narrative on social class in the United States highlights the inequities that exist between the "haves" and the "have-nots," too often oversimplifying and homogenizing the experiences of both groups. Yet the mothers and fathers who participated in my project were far from a homogenous group. Some loved their jobs, while others hated them. Some worked too many hours, others too few. Some had great autonomy at work and experienced tremendous satisfaction on the job, while others felt overly supervised, bored, and frustrated. I saw some families manage this transition beautifully, while others, quite literally, split apart. By focusing exclusively on low-income families, I was able to better understand how and why some low-income families thrive and others falter. Doing so also provides a new lens for evaluating how both policies and interventions designed to support working parents are relevant and effective for low-income families.

Second, I examined these work-family challenges during a critical time in families' lives—the birth of child. Although there is a vast literature on the transition to parenthood, little of this literature examines the second transition most parents experience, that of returning to paid work soon after birth. Even less of that research addresses the experiences of low-income parents as they make these transitions. Relatedly, this project is distinctive in that it looks outside the family, to the workplace, as a critical social setting that shapes child development. Given the latest research identifying the first years of life as fundamental to healthy child development, along with the low probability that low-wage jobs in the United States are going to disappear any time soon, it is imperative that we identify the work conditions under which parents experience positive mental health and children thrive.

Finally, my approach to understanding these challenges relied on information from multiple family members—mothers, fathers, and children—as well as teachers, to explore the short-term and long-term implications of low-wage work for parents and children. By following families over a six-year period, from pregnancy to when their child entered the first grade, I am able to describe different pathways connecting work to child outcomes. Ultimately, the hope is that these numbers and stories will highlight the specific ways in which good, low-wage jobs can enhance parental well-being and child development, and inform policies at workplace, state, and federal levels to bring about the best supports we can provide for low-wage families.

Following families over an extended period of time also allowed my team to capture the ever-changing dynamics of family life, and nothing brings these changes to light more than the real stories of parents living through these transitions. The story of Maria and Carlos, introduced at the beginning of this chapter, illustrates not only the particular challenges of making a living and becoming a parent on limited income, but also the surprising twist and turns that emerge as new parents find their way.

## Maria and Carlos: The Rest of the Story

My second interview with Maria and Carlos took place four weeks after their baby, Matilde, was born. The aim of this interview was to hear about the birth, monitor how things were going, and see if Maria and Carlos had started to plan for their return to work. I sat down to start my conversation with Maria and noticed how tired she looked. As she cradled Matilde in her arms, she shared with me every detail of the birth, from her water breaking to the crowning of her baby's head. According to Maria, "It went well, just long. My water broke on Sunday afternoon, and she wasn't born until Monday evening, but once I had an epidural it got so much better. Carlos was there the entire time, and he was great. It was so much more than either of us expected. She came out, and it was just overwhelming. Just love. Carlos decided to come home with us, and he has been here ever since."

We started talking about their future plans. She told me that Carlos had taken a second job and quit school to help make ends meet, so she could stay home with the baby longer. Their latest plan was that Maria would take care of Matilde, as well as care for her sister's two children, for which her sister would pay her. Her mother was allowing her and Carlos to stay with her while they saved some money for an apartment, and Maria said the birth had brought her and Carlos closer together. She was hopeful. Carlos was also optimistic. "Being a dad is just amazing. She is totally dependent on us and so cute." He told me how he still had his part-time job at the deli, but he was also working more than thirty hours per week at McDonalds. He was tired but also proud that he was providing for his family.

The third interview, which was set to occur after new mothers had been back at work for about a month, allowed us to learn how the first few weeks of this second transition had gone. By this time, Matilde was four months old, and things were not going well. Maria was tired and stressed. The baby wasn't sleeping at night, and, during the day, Maria was caring for her sister's two boys, who were four and two, as well as the baby. "You have no idea how crazy two little boys can be. They aren't good nappers, so I never get a break. My mother and Carlos think that because I am the one that is home I should be doing laundry and keeping the house clean. Yeah, right." As I talked with Maria, my graduate student was interviewing Carlos in the kitchen. He was equally exhausted working two jobs and getting little sleep at night. Both were struggling, and their responses to our questionnaires confirmed our concerns: both parents had depression levels above the clinical cutoff on our standardized measure, indicating they were at risk for clinical depression, and both were reporting high levels of relationship conflict. Carlos wondered out loud if it would be better if he moved back home for a time to give the two of them a break from each other, but he was worried about leaving the baby. They had also had little success saving money for an apartment, as their income went almost entirely to formula, diapers, rent, gas, and other requirements of daily life. Maria was feeling hopeless. "We try to save, and then the car needs a new starter. Formula costs a fortune. And I am stuck at home with three babies." As we said our good-byes, my graduate student and I wished them well and said we would be in touch when Matilde turned six months old.

At the six-month mark, couples filled out questionnaires that we sent in the mail. Soon after Maria returned her questionnaire, I received a teary phone call from her. Carlos had moved back to his mother's house. Her mother and sister disliked having him in the house, and there had been a lot of conflict, so he left. Maria was also miserable in her role as a child-care provider and had informed her sister that she wanted to find a "real" job. According to Maria, the tension in her house was palpable. Her sister was angry with her for changing her mind about child care, while her mother chastised her for not maintaining the house. Maria felt completely isolated. Her depressive symptoms had escalated well above the clinical cutoff for depression. "I am not sure how I got here, but something has to change. I love the baby, but, to be honest, it is hard to get up every day to the same thing. I don't really have anyone to talk to." Meanwhile, Carlos was not faring much better. He missed Maria and

Matilde. His mother had convinced him to quit his job at Mc-Donalds in order to go back to school, and he still had dreams that he could get a better job with an associate's degree, which would allow him to afford an apartment. Unfortunately, his reduced income meant that he was giving Maria less money for the baby, creating even more friction between them. Both Maria and Carlos talked about being at the "breaking point." Things were dire.

I had low expectations when I called, six months later, to set up the final, in-person interview with Maria and Carlos at the twelve-month mark; I was surprised to learn that Maria and Matilde had joined Carlos in his mother's house. Holding a beautiful, brown-eyed baby girl wearing a pink shirt with the words "Daddy's Princess" on the front, Carlos greeted us at the door for our interview. Maria walked in with a big smile on her face and said, "What a difference, huh?" She may have been referring to Matilde, but the difference was noticeable in the parents as well. They were smiling, warm, and relaxed.

Much had happened in six short months. Maria's best friend, who was making $12 an hour caring for a woman who had suffered a stroke, had encouraged Maria to become trained as a home health aide. The certification required seventy-five hours of training, including sixteen hours of practicum, and Carlos, his mother, and Maria's mother all helped care for Matilde during Maria's training. After completing her training, Maria immediately landed a job caring for an older man recovering from hip replacement, as well as one caring for a woman recovering from a stroke. She found the work extremely rewarding. Her clients were friendly and appreciative, and she felt a degree of independence and purpose at work that she had never felt before. "It feels good to get out in the world. When I come home, I really have missed Matilde, but I know she is fine. I know I am a better mom, and to be honest, I am just a nicer person." Importantly, Maria's depression score had dropped well below the clinical cutoff. She had full-time work with a consistent eight-to-four schedule, as well as some weekend work. Since Carlos often worked during the evenings and weekends, they were able to work out some opposite shift hours, and they used a family day care for about fifteen to twenty hours per week. Finances remained tight, but they were managing, in part, thanks to the support from Carlos's mother, who was charging them only $200 each month to live with her.

Carlos was also doing better. While he was still frustrated about his low-paying work at the deli, he needed only four more courses to complete his associate's degree and was feeling hopeful about finishing school. His depression scores had also dropped below the clinical level. He reported that he and Maria were fighting less and going on occasional dates to the movies and out to dinner. They had even begun to talk about marriage. As Carlos said with a chuckle, "To be continued."

This ending is hardly the one we see portrayed in the popular press about low-income, unmarried parents, and, of course, it is hardly "an ending." It is also only one story of many in our project. Some couples have an easier course, some harder. Some stay together; some separate. For both Maria and Carlos, work played a critical role in how the year went. Maria found a job she enjoyed and learned that she was a better parent and partner when she had the opportunity to leave the house and engage with others. The pay was still too low, but the job left her feeling good about herself, rather than depleted; she could come home and be an engaged mother. Once Carlos returned to school, he felt hopeful about the future. He could handle his minimum-wage job at the deli knowing that he was working toward a degree that would get him a "real job." Of course,

Maria and Carlos could pull this off only with the help and support of their families—a consistent theme in our study. If new parents have a support network, they fare much better on all counts than those with no support. What else have we learned from the experiences of new parents like Maria and Carlos?

## What We've Learned and What We Might Do

Perhaps the most important lesson learned during this study is that our efforts to improve and sustain the healthy development of children in this country cannot focus solely on how well parents care for their young—an approach that places the full onus of the well-being of the next generation on the shoulders of parents alone. Job conditions, workplace policies, parental leave policies, and child care create a complex web of resources and limitations that directly shape working parents' ability to care for their children. The right combination of circumstances and policies can lead to positive outcomes for parents and their children, while the wrong combination can be toxic. While I describe these conditions in detail over the course of the following chapters, I want to highlight a few general findings at the outset, before briefly describing the road ahead.

One recurrent theme is that small interventions can make a big difference. For instance, simply having twelve weeks of leave, along with some minimal scheduling flexibility—like being able to leave work for a doctor's appointment—resulted in positive implications for new mothers' mental health. Similarly, when mothers faced looming deadlines or had productivity goals to meet, a supportive supervisor buffered the effects of this stress. Mothers in high-pressure jobs with unsupportive supervisors, by contrast, had not only higher levels of depression but depression that worsened over time. Dealing with a stressful job with little support from a supervisor proved very costly for working mothers.

Another central finding is that work experiences matter for parenting. Job conditions—whether coworker relations, amount of control and autonomy at work, or levels of job stress—affect the ability of parents to care for their children. A lack of autonomy in the workplace, for example, led mothers to report a more generalized lack of control and efficacy in their life, which we found resulted in a decline in parenting quality. By contrast, we found that when employees are satisfied with their jobs, even if demanding and stressful, it can spill over to home life and result in higher-quality parenting. As we will see, the pathways through which work influences a person's ability to parent can be both direct and indirect and are often complex, but the evidence of their impact is undeniable.

Finally, the evidence suggests that, for both mothers and fathers, work experiences during the first year of their child's life were related to the child's behavioral outcomes six years later. For instance, when mothers and fathers experienced a sense of control and efficacy at work during the transition to parenthood, their children displayed better social skills and fewer behavioral problems in the first grade. These long-term effects point to the salience of the first year of life in setting the stage for both parents and children.

As I have presented our findings over the years at conferences and policy meetings, almost everyone I have spoken with agrees that we need to provide better support to working parents, but the big concern is always the price tag. How can we afford to institute policies at the federal, state, and workplace levels? As one legislator said to me, "We are the richest most successful country in the world because we don't act like our people need our help. They can do it alone; Americans always have." In fact, Americans have never "done it alone," and what we are doing now, having both parents work full-time with barely a break for childbirth, is relatively new territory in this country, a social experiment only about fifty years in the making. Nor is it true that new policies are unaffordable. Some states have already started to institute one of the costliest of policies—paid parental leave—and early data suggest it is a "win-win" for employers and employees. As the findings above indicate, other potential interventions—such as increased flexibility, supportive supervisors, and positive work environments—are surprisingly affordable, and, here again, data suggest, result in less employee turnover, better employee health, and fewer sick days. I will return to these possible solutions in the final chapter of the book, but first we have much to learn about the challenges and rewards of becoming a parent in the United States while holding down a low-wage job.

In the following chapter, I look at what we know about social class, and how income, education, and occupational status shape the transition to parenthood. I also provide a deeper dive into the study itself by describing the sample, our data collection procedures, and the rationale for focusing exclusively on low-income families. In chapter 3, I address workplace policies, such as paid leave, flexible schedules, and sick time, as they relate to the well-being of new parents. I couple quantitative findings with a number of stories that bring to light the pain that unsupportive policies inflict, and the relief that even minimal workplace supports can offer new parents. Chapter 4 turns from the importance of workplace policies to the importance of job conditions. I explore how various aspects of one's job—including stress, autonomy, and workplace relationships—can shape parental well-being across the first year of parenthood. In chapter 5, I discuss the role that work policies and job conditions play in the quality of parenting that employed mothers and fathers provide to their new infants. I describe, in particular, how stressful work can impinge on parents' abilities to be sensitive and responsive caregivers to their new infants. In chapter 6, I turn to the long-term impact of parents' work experiences on children's development and explain the direct and indirect pathways through which parental work influences children's social and cognitive outcomes. In the final chapter, I provide an overview of the lessons I have learned from this project and draw on these lessons to formulate recommendations for policy makers, employers, and researchers.

Much has been written about the challenges of managing work and family life. These challenges are not fairly distributed, nor are they always obvious. In the following pages, I lay out the myriad ways that parents' jobs can affect them, their parenting, and their children. As you will see, things do not always go as we might expect. Supervisors intervene, promotions happen, coworkers help out, workers are fired, and schedules change. These experiences are then carried home, where they affect workers' well-being, relationships, and children, for better or worse.

# CHAPTER 2

# "The Invisible Americans"

## *The Work and Family Transitions Project*

"Have you ever seen that picture of the American dream? There is this race track, and at the end is a sign saying, 'the American dream,' and all these racers are lined up to get to the dream, but the thing is they all have different starting lines. That is my life, and it is sadly so true and not fair. My parents couldn't afford to send me to college. It wasn't even an option. How am I supposed to win the race?" This was the explanation offered to me by Cheyenne, a young Black woman who worked as a waitress at a breakfast diner, as to why she was stuck in her "dead-end" job. She was angry and bitter about her situation, feelings shared by many parents. Although we never directly asked parents about social class or inequality, they frequently raised the topics while describing the challenges they faced. They talked about unequal pay, the "haves and the have-nots," "blue-collar work," "uppity supervisors," "White trash," and the "one-percenters." The explanations they offered for the existence of income and educational inequalities encompassed a wide range of attitudes. Peter, a long-distance truck driver who listened to Fox News podcasts on his rides, told me, "We are a classless society." In contrast to Cheyenne's assessment, which pinpointed unfair starting lines as the source of inequality, Peter believed that "it only takes hard work and commitment to make it in this world. People have gotten soft and lazy."

Issues of opportunity and hard work only become more salient when contemplating our children's future. Most parents I talked with wanted their children to attend good schools, to graduate college, and to find meaningful, high-paying jobs. As Kai, a young father who worked in the cafeteria at a local college, described his dreams for his four-week-old baby, "I want her to have a good life, a great life. I don't want her treated like a second-class citizen like me. Those college kids at work don't even see me. . . . I want her to be the college kid."

Matters of social class lie at the heart of this inquiry. In this project, my team and I followed a sample of low-income, working families in order to understand how parents in this particular economic stratum coped with the demands of work and family. Since work-family issues affect everyone, I am often asked: Why did you only focus on low-income families in your project? Why didn't you have a comparison group of middle-class families? What about poor families? These are good questions, and in this chapter, I explain why I chose to concentrate on the experiences of low-income families, why I decided to focus on the transition to parenthood, and why it is so important to follow families over an extended period of time. In addition to explaining the underlying motivations for the project, I also describe in greater detail how we actually carried out this study, who participated, the types of data we collected, and some of the challenges we encountered along the way. This chapter serves as an important prologue to the stories and results that follow because it demonstrates the depth, rigor, and originality of the research on which those findings are based.

## The Meaning of Social Class

All of us—academics, government officials, politicians, reporters, the general public—use notions of social class to understand and explain how our world works. We are often acutely aware of who stands "above" and "below" us in the class hierarchy. But what is social class, and why does it matter? Most researchers agree that social class refers to social categories in our society that are based, in some way, on a combination of education, occupational status, income, and wealth. Social class matters because these factors shape our social reality, as well as our beliefs, values, and behaviors.[1] [2] In his classic book *Class and Conformity*, Melvin Kohn argues that social class is compelling because "it captures the reality that the intricate interplay of all these variables (i.e., income, education, occupation)] creates different levels of the social order. Members of different social classes, by virtue of enjoying (or suffering) different conditions of life come to see the world differently—to develop different conceptions of social reality, different aspirations and hopes and fears, different conceptions of the desirable."[3]

I set out to understand how families in the lower levels of the US class system, primarily working-class families, experienced parenthood and work, not in comparison to their more privileged counterparts, but in their own right. What similarities and differences exist in the experiences of low-income families? How do differences in resources, opportunities, and supports within low-income jobs affect parents' ability to manage parenting responsibilities and the development of their children? For example, within low-wage occupations, to what extent do demanding, stressful, or supportive interactions with a supervisor influence a worker's interactions with his or her child at home? Does having friends at work make the workday better, and does this experience spill over in positive ways to home life? In taking this approach, I made the assumption that there existed variability in the conditions and experiences of low-wage jobs, and that these variations would affect workers' family lives in positive and negative ways. I wanted to understand how parents' work life creeps into their life outside of work, in obvious and in hidden ways. Once we understand the pathways linking work to family life, we can use that information to provide direction for developing policies and programs to support working parents.

The existing literature on social class is enormous and messy. Classifications and definitions of class are imprecise, at best, and biased at worst. There are no agreed-on guidelines that distinguish working-class families from middle-class or poor families. In fact, the Census Bureau avoids any discussion of social class and simply reports income, wealth, and education levels. Nevertheless, despite the fact that the term "social class" is fraught with ambiguity, researchers continue to use it as an organizing concept because it has utility. Indexes of education, income, and prestige, used alone or in some combination, distinguish class categories; and these class categories serve as important proxies for privilege, power, inequality, discrimination, and opportunity in our society.

While academics may never reach consensus about just what social class is, in the real world almost anyone you talk to can describe what social class means. Whatever their walk of life, people tend to agree that the experiences of the "upper class" differ from those of the "middle class" or the "working class" in terms of opportunities, values, and resources. But what difference does a label really make? According to Lillian Rubin, a well-known scholar of social class, most Americans see themselves as "middle class," which is one reason much of our public discourse focuses on middle-class Americans. Often the experiences of working families, who are poor or near poor, are subsumed into middle-class narratives, rendering their circumstances invisible. As Rubin has argued, "if the popular political language denies the very existence of a sector of the population [e.g., the working class], their needs are not likely to be taken into account."[4]

Rubin's insight is critical. The needs, special circumstances, and unique challenges facing working families who are hovering near or even somewhat above poverty are markedly different from those facing families earning above the median household income. Referring to this broad swath of families as "middle class" masks important differences, which are then easily ignored in policy debates. These working-class families are, in Rubin's words, "invisible Americans."[5] An aim of my study was to make these invisible Americans visible. I wanted to understand the unique challenges facing families holding down low-wage jobs and managing the demands of new parenthood, and in the process highlight specific factors that either support them or make the work-family juggling act untenable.

## The American Class Structure

So how many "invisible Americans" are there? This is an important question because understanding the distribution of social class lets us see exactly how many families are currently living on a precarious financial foundation, where any disruption, an illness or job layoff, could leave them homeless. In their body of work analyzing the American class structure, Dennis Gilbert and Joseph Kahl describe the class distribution in the United States as shaped like a tear drop, with most of the population falling at or below middle class.[6] As Gilbert points out, social

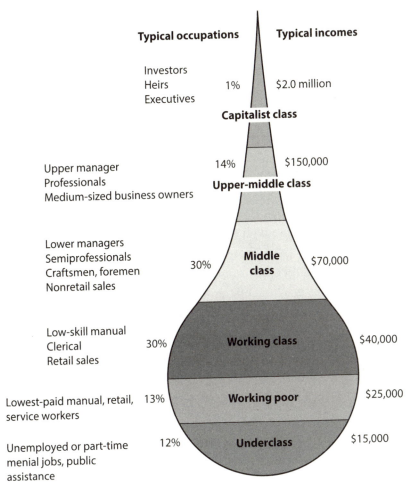

**Typical occupations**

Investors
Heirs
Executives

1%

**Typical incomes**

$2.0 million

**Capitalist class**

Upper manager
Professionals
Medium-sized business owners

14%

$150,000

**Upper-middle class**

Lower managers
Semiprofessionals
Craftsmen, foremen
Nonretail sales

30%

**Middle class**

$70,000

Low-skill manual
Clerical
Retail sales

30%

**Working class**

$40,000

Lowest-paid manual, retail, service workers

13%

**Working poor**

$25,000

Unemployed or part-time menial jobs, public assistance

12%

**Underclass**

$15,000

FIGURE 1. Gilbert-Kahl model of the class structure.

*Source*: Gilbert, Dennis (2014), *The American Class Structure in an Age of Growing Inequality*, Thousand Oaks, CA: SAGE Publications.

class is a moving target because individuals and families regularly move across class levels in response to economic surges and downturns. With that caveat in mind, he categorizes 30 to 35 percent of American workers as working class, while the working poor constitute about 13 percent of workers. Taken together, these two groups make up the largest portion of our society (see figure 1).

These two classes are distinguished from one another primarily on the basis of education. Members of the working class typically hold a high school degree and perhaps some additional certificates or training degrees, while the working poor usually have some high school education but may not hold a high school degree. These educational differences are tied to occupational differences: members of the working class hold such jobs as machine operators, mechanics, clerical workers, nursing assistants, and retail sales workers, while the working poor are most often food service workers, laborers, or low-paid operators and clericals. More recently, research points to the rise of "brown-collar" occupations, especially among Latinos who have recently immigrated. Brown-collar jobs include poorly paid, irregular occupations in the service industries or agriculture.[7]

As I noted earlier, there is significant disagreement over how to define social class. For example, the Urban Institute, a Washington, DC–based think tank that conducts economic and social policy research, defines as "lower middle class" those households with incomes ranging from $30,000 to $49,999.[8] According to this definition, a two-parent family in which both parents are employed in full-time, minimum-wage jobs (federal minimum wage is $7.25 an hour) would barely squeak into the middle class, since their household income would be approximately $30,000 a year.

I argue that definitions of "middle class" are overly broad and obscure important social realities. To see why, consider that the federal poverty guidelines for a family of three in 2021 was $21,960. Based on the guidelines provide by the Urban Institute, a family moves from poverty, at approximately $22,000 a year, to middle class, at around $30,000 a year, with a mere $8,000 increase in family income. Where, according to these definitions, are the working class or working poor? Such expansive understandings of the middle class overlook the distinctive experiences of those families who live above the poverty level but lack the security of families making the median household income in the United States, which currently sits at $65,712.[9] For the purposes of this study, our definition of social class relied on both educational level and income. Specifically, we limited our focus to those with an educational attainment of an associate's degree or less, with the majority of our parents having a high school degree. Using income as an indicator of class was often misleading because many parents, especially fathers, held down two or three jobs at different times, raising their income but rarely their status. Thus, we looked at hourly wages, limiting our focus to those earning between $7.25 and $18.00 an hour, and type of job as indicators of class. Importantly, both mothers and fathers had to fit these criteria to be included in the study.

Another important challenge in defining social class arises from how household and family income are measured by researchers. Specifically, the Census Bureau measures household income as the sum of the income of all persons, fifteen years and older, occupying the same housing unit.[10] Thus, in one family, a mother, father, and grandparent could each be contributing to household income, while in another family one worker could be providing an equivalent household income. This is a critical difference, especially for families with infants and young children. If one person can earn $30,000, it frees up the other person (or persons) in the home to care for children, thereby minimizing or avoiding entirely the high costs of infant care. Conversely, if both parents work full-time minimum-wage jobs, together bringing home $30,000, then the costs of child care will normally need to be covered by that income as well. For the majority of families in our study, if one worker were to drop out of the labor force, the family would be on the brink of poverty or fall into poverty. Most were not living below the poverty level, but close to it, a level at which a family makes too much money for child-care subsidies but too little money to take advantage of tax breaks or saving plans.

Setting aside differences in household income, there are other respects in which the work and family experiences of lower-income working parents are significantly different from those of their more affluent counterparts. These differences, however, are often masked by the ways in which social scientists analyze their data. For example, let's say I want to understand how parents' job autonomy and flexibility are related to the development of their children's social skills. I would ask parents about their autonomy at work and the degree of flexibility they have in their work schedule and then link these assessments to teachers' reports of children's social skills at school. The reasonable hypothesis would be that greater autonomy and more flexibility at work for parents is good for children, no matter parents' income or education. Based on this assumption, researchers would control for these indicators of social class in their analyses, so they could make some global statement about how job flexibility or autonomy relates to children's social skills. There are, however, two key flaws with this approach. First, it neglects to consider how work and family linkages may differ between social classes. In fact, some research shows that flexibility for high-wage workers is good for working parents and their children, while for low-wage workers, "flexibility" at work often translates into fewer and less predictable hours, outcomes that negatively affect families.[11] Simply controlling for social class would hide these different processes. Second, while it may be possible in a statistical analysis to control for key demographic variables, such as income and education, it is not that simple in the real world. If only we could "control" for poverty and low education! Thus, when we explore the relationship between work and family life, it is imperative to pose questions and uncover answers that arise *within* the social, economic, and cultural contexts in which they occur. This is why, in my study, I focused on work and family processes within working-class and working-poor families—what factors shape positive and negative parental and child outcomes among families facing the same economic and job constraints?

## What We Know about Working-Class and Working-Poor Families

The lives of working-class families were quite poignantly portrayed in Mirra Komarovsky's *Blue Collar Marriage* (1962),[12] in which she described the lack of intimacy, marital conflict, and daily struggle that characterized raising a family on meager wages in the 1960s. Fourteen years later, in *Worlds of Pain* (1976),[13] Lillian Rubin painted an equally grim picture of the working-class families who were barely squeaking by financially—buying secondhand clothes for their kids, repairing cars on their last legs, and going into debt with no time or money for fun and leisure. In light of the dramatically shifting social, economic, and political changes that occurred between the 1970s and 1990s, Rubin revisited working-class families in her book *Families on the Fault Line* (1994).[14] In this latter work, she explored how frustrations borne of financial stress and economic inequality are often directed at racial and ethnic conflicts, rather than toward an economic system that constrains and harms low-income families. These authors were the first to shed light on the inner worlds of working-class families while highlighting how inequities in our economic and social systems create undue pressure on those at the lower end of the economic spectrum. How are the families that Komarovsky and Rubin studied in the twentieth century faring in the twenty-first century?

Much has been learned about low-income families over the past decade. Numerous studies and books point to declining "real wages," precarious jobs, unpredictable job schedules, social isolation, and decreases in government support programs.[15] [16] [17] [18] Challenges facing low-income families in the United States have been steadily increasing, while the safety nets are vanishing, leading to what some have referred to as the abandonment of our most vulnerable families.[19] [20] Research by Kathryn Edin and Luke Schaefer, for instance, has described the experiences of individuals subsisting on less than $2.00 a day, despite having sporadic ties to the labor market.[21]

The families in this study were not facing such dire circumstances. The majority of parents we interviewed had stable, if meager, living arrangements. Most lived in an apartment, either by themselves or sometimes with other family members. As my team and I followed them over time, some lost their jobs, hit hard times, and landed in shelters or on friends' couches. Few were officially poor, but most struggled financially. All were facing the huge financial and emotional challenges of new parenthood.

# The Transition to Parenthood among Low-Income Families

Researchers have been studying the transition to parenthood for decades, most often addressing how having a baby affects the quality of parents' intimate relationships, their well-being, and their children's well-being. The first studies on the transition to parenthood characterized it as a time of "crisis" in relationships, which resulted in conflict and dissatisfaction.[22] [23] Over the years, this depiction has softened: the transition is now characterized as a normative life event, one that creates some instability, but from which most parents recover.[24] On average, new parents experience an increase in stress, a decrease in well-being, and more relationship conflict early in the transition, but they tend to recover significantly over the first year. What we see "on average," however, masks the great variability in couples' experiences: some individuals and couples remain fairly stable in terms of their mental health and relationship satisfaction throughout the transition, some do better over time, and some decline precipitously on both counts. What we want to know is why some parents do well, while others struggle. What predicts these differences in parents' outcomes?

Numerous factors affect how well parents cope with new parenthood: parents' mental health and relationship quality prior to the birth, social support, child temperament, financial resources, and the division of household tasks and child care.[25] Many studies point to the ways in which these factors affect how well parents function during the transition to parenthood, yet few examine work as a key factor shaping the transition. Moreover, as I mentioned in the previous chapter, much of what we know about this transition is based on middle-class, White families. We don't know if the same patterns hold among working-class and working-poor families, who manage this transition in the face of vastly different financial circumstances.

Only a handful of studies on the transition to parenthood consider how the return to work or the conditions of a job affect parents' well-being. We do know that low-income mothers return to paid work far sooner after birth than more affluent mothers because low-income mothers rarely have access to paid leave benefits and often cannot afford to take unpaid leave. We also know that new mothers and fathers who have to return to work soon after birth are often emotionally and physically depleted. It should therefore not come as a surprise that among low-income women, the incidence of maternal depression in the months just before and after childbirth is as high as one in four (much higher than the already high one in seven mothers in the general population). Postnatal depression creates long-term risks for mothers' future mental health and their children's healthy development. Specifically, maternal depression is related to a higher incidence of problem behaviors and greater anxiety in children and poorer academic achievement for them. One way that mothers' depression is transmitted to their children, which chapter 5 examines in depth, is through impaired parenting, where a mother may disengage from her child or be unable to provide warmth and nurturance.

Far less is known about how fathers' work is related to mental health, parenting, and children's development. As a society, we have spent decades debating the pros and cons of mothers' employment for everything from children's attachment relationships to their mental health and academic achievement. In this vast literature, fathers and their work have been largely absent. In fact, more has been written about the effects of fathers' unemployment on children and families than about their employment. As we will see in the following chapters, fathers' work matters as much for children as mothers' work.

There is also, to date, little research that connects the conditions experienced by new parents in low-wage jobs to the health and development of their children. Compared to the influence of certain formal features of a job—wages, hours, leaves, and schedules—we know far less about how parents' experiences on the job during the early months of parenting affect them and their children. However, a few studies offer some clues. One recent study, for instance, points to the role of supervisors. In fascinating research by the psychologist Anna Gassman-Pines, low-income mothers who experience criticism from their supervisors were found to be more withdrawn at home. After returning from work, they tended to pull back from parenting activities. On the other hand, supervisor recognition and support was related to warmer parenting behavior.[26] Similarly, in a rare study of low-income fathers, conducted by family scientist Ben Goodman and colleagues, it was found that having a supportive work environment resulted in more sensitive parenting.[27] In a separate study, Gassman-Pines (2015) discovered that on days when parents experience discrimination at work, both mothers and fathers reported worse moods at home. In addition, when fathers experienced discrimination on the job, their children tended to display higher levels of problem behaviors (e.g., aggression, sadness).[28] These recent findings provide evidence that what happens at work matters for parenting and, therefore, matters for children's development. Questions remain, however, as to how the timing and duration of these experiences affect children.

Thus, in this project I decided to start at the very beginning—during pregnancy—and follow the families as their children grew up. Based on insights from the literature, I set out to conduct a study that followed families from pregnancy across the first year of life to witness, in real time, how new parents cope with caring for an infant and managing work demands. With additional funding, we then followed these families into the first grade. I also chose to focus in on families employed in low-wage jobs, the largest group of new parents in the United States, but a group we know the least about. Finally, I was interested in how both parents' jobs, not just those of mothers, shaped the health and well-being of parents and their children during the first year of life but also as children develop over time. To my knowledge, this is one of the first studies of early child development that focuses on how characteristics of parents' jobs shape parents' and children's well-being from birth to the first grade.

## A Readers' Guide to the Work and Family Transitions Project (WFTP)

The families who participated in this study lived and worked in and around Springfield, Massachusetts, the third largest city in the state. While Massachusetts has a reputation for being a progressive state with good health-care policies and family supports, at the time of this study the state did not offer paid leave for pregnancy or birth. Springfield is a sprawling city, whose thirteen neighborhoods have significant racial and ethnic diversity. Springfield is also a relatively poor city. Almost half of all children in Springfield live in poverty, and its overall poverty rate hovers around 30 percent, more than double the national average. In the first decade of the century, when this project started, Springfield had one of the highest crime rates in the country for a midsized city,[29] although efforts by the mayor and police department over the past decade have been successful in reducing these rates. As happens with many longitudinal studies, economic and social events had unintended effects on our research. Most significantly, some of the families in the study were severely affected by the economic recession of 2008 and

2009. The families were already struggling financially, and the recession resulted in many of the parents becoming unemployed or experiencing significant job insecurity. The stress of the recession is reflected in many of the parents' stories of financial struggles and parenting.

The 360 families that took part in this project shared some key features: as the study began, they were expecting a child, and they worked and were planning to continue working after the birth. The majority of participants had graduated from high school, and some had vocational and technical training, and none had completed college. Income varied quite significantly across families because, as we quickly learned, many of the fathers and a few of the mothers held down two or three jobs. (Full details and sample descriptive statistics can be found in appendix A.)

The most common jobs for mothers were nursing aide, food service worker, and beautician; for fathers, they were truck driver, laborer, and maintenance worker. Median salaries were $30,237 ($14.53 an hour) for men, and $25,320 ($12.17 an hour) for women, and the median family income was $43,607. (These estimates represent gross income; after taxes, take home pay was significantly less.) In addition, roughly one-third of fathers and one-tenth of mothers held a second job. On average, fathers worked an additional nine hours per week in their second job, while mothers worked about four additional hours.

All families participated in a series of five interviews that extended from pregnancy through one year postpartum, and families were interviewed again as their child entered the first grade. During in-home interviews, we collected survey data on parents' work conditions, mental health, relationship quality, gender ideology, parenting behaviors, and stress levels. We also collected data on parent-child relations and, later on, had parents and teachers report on children's socioemotional outcomes, such as their ability to manage and express emotions and sustain positive relationships, and cognitive outcomes, such as literacy skills, math ability, and problem solving. We also interviewed children themselves. Over the years, as we visited and revisited families, our project slowly turned into something more immersive, meaning we went beyond the questionnaires and protocols to simply hear from family members about their experiences. We wanted to hear their stories. As we came to know these families, we realized it was important to describe their experiences and learn from their insights about how things were going.

Some version of this clean, straightforward, uncomplicated picture of the families who participated in the study appears in every one of our published papers. But the clean pictures that academics present in research articles do not usually reflect the messy and challenging nature of social research. Both our recruitment and our interview processes changed as we came to recognize oversights, mistakes, biases, and blind spots. Below, I briefly lay out some of the major issues that led to changes in the ways we interacted with families. This information provides a more complete picture of who was included, and who was not. It also explains why some aspects of the study did not go as we had originally planned and acknowledges how the mothers, fathers, and children who participated both informed and, at times, changed our approach.

First, our study became a mixed-methods project—meaning that it combined both qualitative and quantitative approaches—almost immediately after our conducting the first pilot interviews. As we went into family homes and started having parents fill out questionnaire after questionnaire, we realized we were missing something important. We were not capturing the details and stories that they were sharing with us. For example, after

Wendy filled out the Edinburgh Depression Scale as part of the interview, she turned to me with tears in her eyes and described how worried she was about leaving her baby to go to work. "Will she remember I am her real mom? It just makes me so sad. Will she resent me later?" The fact that our depression scale was triggering her worries about motherhood and work was important and needed to be captured. In response, we added open-ended questions throughout the interview in order to give parents the opportunity to share their feelings and thoughts. Their stories provide the context and meaning behind our numbers.

Recruitment presented another immediate challenge. At the outset, we were having a great deal of trouble recruiting low-income families. I quickly found out why that was the case. The original study design called for married parents who were having their first child and employed full-time in low-wage jobs. These inclusion criteria excluded the majority of expectant parents who were unwed in the city of Springfield, a city that had a 34 percent marriage rate, with the lowest rates occurring in low-income households. I had inadvertently designed a study that eliminated a huge swath of low-income families. This was a significant flaw caused by my own blind spots and biases, which had to be corrected. In collaboration with my co-investigator Joyce Everett, a scholar at Smith College who studied risk and resilience among African-American families, we stepped back and rethought our approach to recruitment not only around social class but around race and ethnicity. We partnered with churches and community centers, shared our findings with families along the way, and developed respectful and sustained relationships with community leaders. We also wrote a new grant aimed at better reflecting the experiences of those families I had excluded in the original design.[30] The second wave of recruitment included married, cohabiting, and single-mother families, and it added to the study fairly equal numbers of Black, Latino, and White families, markedly increasing the racial and ethnic diversity of families in the study. As will be shown in later chapters, although we did uncover some differences in mental health indexes based on race and ethnicity, the processes linking work to parent mental health and parenting and child outcomes did not differ for Black, White, or Latino families.

We also faced difficulties determining the appropriate measures to use in the study. As I have pointed out, most of the prior research had focused on middle-class, White families, so we could not be sure that the measures or questions previously relied on would be relevant or valid for our participants of color and for lower-income households. For example, since one of our primary aims was to understand the work experiences of parents, we asked many questions about their jobs. We began by asking parents questions that we thought would have fairly straightforward answers, such as "How many hours do you work in a week?" and "What is your work schedule?" As we soon discovered, these turned out to be tricky and sensitive questions for many participants.

We interviewed mothers and fathers separately and asked both parents about their own jobs, work hours, and income, as well as those of their partners. We soon began to notice discrepancies in what couples told us. For example, Caleb reported working as a welder for forty hours per week, with sporadic overtime. His wife, Leigh, however, told me that Caleb worked about fifty-four hours per week. A fourteen-hour difference seemed significant and puzzling. Luckily, since we went back to visit families every few months, we were able to address the discrepancies in reporting. We quickly learned that husbands, more than wives, were underreporting their work hours. Caleb actually had a second job, where he worked "under the table" for an extra twelve to fourteen hours per week (all day Saturday and a few hours on two evenings each week). We found out that many fathers in our study had second and third "under-the-table" jobs. They were paid in cash, and their incomes were not reported. Not surprisingly, they were extremely hesitant to report these jobs to us for fear that we would report this information to the IRS. Going forward, we changed our approach and prefaced all questions about income and work hours with a reminder that their responses were confidential and their individual data would never be shared with outside sources. Slowly, as families began to trust us, the "real" stories started to emerge. By the one-year follow-up interview, far more husbands reported working multiple jobs that were not "on the books," and their work hours increased by an average of 15 to 20 percent between the first and last interview. It is reasonable to conclude that these same measurement issues exist in our national workforce data sets and, therefore, that our estimates of work hours and income for low-income workers may be significantly deflated.

Asking low-income workers about work hours was challenging for additional reasons: many workers held multiple jobs, seasonal jobs, or unstable jobs with hours that varied week to week or month to month. For example, Paco worked at his parents' restaurant about thirty hours per week as a line cook. He usually worked a long shift on Saturday (twelve hours) and three shorter shifts during the week (eighteen hours over three days). Paco also worked almost full-time for his uncle's landscaping business during the summer and plowed snow in the winter. In addition, he sporadically worked at his cousin's car-detailing business. Thus, depending on the season and week, Paco's hours varied between thirty and seventy per week, which of course dramatically affected his income as well. Our estimates of his work hours and the stability of his hours, income, and schedule were simply inadequate to reflect this amount of variability. To address this shortcoming, we began to ask about monthly schedules and would often pore over calendars and schedules with families. None of these numbers could completely capture Paco's work experiences, nor how they influenced his family life. The qualitative stories described in the following chapters provide important examples of how work has become a nearly 24/7 endeavor for many low-wage workers, a reality that impinges on every aspect of family life.

In sharing these challenges, I do not intend to call into question the results of the study, or to offer excuses for what we did and did not study. Rather, I want readers to appreciate the depth of our data: the opportunities we took to go "off script" to learn new things, as well as the rigor and in-depth analyses we used to blend our quantitative and qualitative data. Research in the field is exciting, often in the moment, and, at times, very hard to "control" in a scientific sense. Studies become complicated by these challenges, but as a result, they are richer in their findings and implications. Again and again, the "averages" and "trends" that are described in so many academic papers, my own as well, fail to capture how and why the relationship between the transition to parenthood and work can go so well for some and be such a nightmare for others. In the following chapters, we use families' stories as they unfold over time to provide examples, recommendations, and warnings from parents themselves about how to manage the world of parenthood as a low-wage worker.

# CHAPTER 3

# "A Little Can Go a Long Way"

*Workplace Policies and Parents' Well-Being*

The crisis hit when Lyla was at work. She was an aide in a group home for young adults with developmental disabilities and had been helping a client make lunch when her water broke unexpectedly, two and half months early. Her coworkers rushed her to the hospital, but attempts to slow down the labor were unsuccessful. Her son, Jaylen, was born three hours later, tiny but alive. As Lyla shared with me, "It's been hard since then. Jaylen was born ten weeks early, and he was only three pound, eight ounces, so he had to stay in the hospital. I needed to be home when he got out, so I had to go back to work right away, four days later . . . to save my leave time for when I could take him home. That felt awful." With only twelve weeks of unpaid leave, Layla could not afford to use up her leave to stay with her son before he was released from the hospital.

Policy debates and legislative battles often seem far removed from everyday life. Yet, in reality, policies related to parental leave, sick time, personal time, and minimum wage directly and continuously influence the lives of families, as Lyla's story illustrates. Lyla's experience also highlights the far more dramatic effects that the lack of workplace supports can have on low-wage workers. In the United States, despite the lack of a national paid parental leave policy, many professional workers have access to some paid leave and often possess other financial assets, which they can utilize in a crisis. Low-income families have no such cushion.[1] The financial necessity to return to work within weeks of an infant's birth, the lack of paid sick time or personal time to care for an ill infant, and unpredictable work schedules that make it impossible to plan predictable child care are just some of the challenges faced by low-wage, working parents.

Will these work conditions, in addition to being heartless and unfair, have any long-term, negative effects on Lyla and her baby? Do short parental leaves affect parents' mental health? Does that lack of full-time parental care in the early weeks of an infant's life hold long-term implications for a child's development? This chapter explores these questions by looking at how the more "structural" aspects of parents' work—job schedules, hours, leave benefits, and flexibility—relate to parents' mental health. Some of what we found is predictable. Almost universally, parents reported minimal work-family supports on the job. Only a handful had any type of paid leave, and even those eligible for unpaid leave could rarely use the full twelve weeks offered through the federal Family and Medical Leave Act (FMLA). Nevertheless, we found that even slightly longer leaves (twelve weeks compared to less than six) and even a small degree of flexibility in schedules boded well for mothers' mental health. Fathers also reported less anxiety when mothers were able to take longer leaves, as well as when they had more access to child-care supports. These results, which focus on parents' mental health, are important for children as well as parents. Children rarely experience their parents' work directly but instead experience parents who are affected by their jobs, for better or worse. Thus, workplace policies and conditions are most likely to affect children through their parents' well-being, which is one reason it is critical to focus on parents' psychological health after birth.

Studies show that 45 to 65 percent of depressed women experience their first depressive episode during their first pregnancy or postpartum year.[2] This means that perinatal depression, which is depression that occurs during pregnancy up through the first year after birth, often sets the stage for later mental health problems. Maternal depression also has long-lasting, negative effects on children's cognitive, emotional, and physical development.[3] [4] When infants are cared for by depressed mothers, they often receive adequate physical care but deficient emotional care, as mothers may be withdrawn and exhibit a "flatness" in their responses to their children. This lack of maternal warmth and connection can result in adverse physical reactions in infants, which can include disruptions in the way their bodies manage stress. Such disruptions can lead to emotional distress and dysregulation in infants that can compromise the healthy development of the infant brain.[5] The data on fathers' mental health are much thinner, but there is some research linking paternal depression to poorer parenting quality as well.[6] This research makes evident the importance of parents' mental health to early child development. It also gives us reason to investigate how low-wage work affects workers' mental health, especially during the sensitive period surrounding the birth of a baby.

In the hundreds of hours that we spent talking to new parents about their birth experiences and return to paid work, we heard story after story about their struggles. Most stories were not as dramatic as Lyla's, but many were still heart wrenching. For example, Tamara, a twenty-four-year-old medical assistant, described the problems caused by the lack of flexibility in her job. "The difficult part is how rigid it is. So that makes it hard on you; so their inflexibility is what makes it hard on you. Just being pregnant with appointments and all, and them not wanting to give even a little bit. Like I was willing to make up hours on my day off or not take a lunch all week so I could go to an appointment. It was an appointment that wasn't planned, so you know, it's just people not willing to work with you or stuff like that." Jean had a similar story to tell. She worked as a grocery store clerk and was told that, during her four-hour shifts, she wasn't allowed to sit down on a stool between customers, despite being in her third trimester of pregnancy.

Many parents talked about the rigid rules and regulations that supervisors referred to when denying them some small request. As one supervisor told Kyle, a factory worker, "Sorry I can't help, but them's the rules." The stringent conditions Kyle described were common in many workplaces: "If you call in less than eight hours before your shift, you get a black mark. If you say your kid has to go to the dentist or is sick and your wife can't cover it, and you haven't given proper notice, you get a black mark. Then after five marks you get a verbal warning, six a written warning, seven you get a final warning, and eight you are fired." Employees could also get "black marks" for taking a personal day if it was not approved ahead of time, for coming in late, or for leaving early. Kyle said that he rarely incurred any black marks until he had a baby. "Once you have a kid, sometimes things just get complicated, and you run late."

Another challenge described by many of the parents was mandatory overtime, a policy whereby employers require employees to work more than forty hours per week—what many workers accurately referred to as "forced overtime." New parents would be told, on very short notice, that they needed to work late to complete a work order, or to cover for the absence of a coworker. If employees refused the mandatory overtime, their employer might dock them a day's pay or a vacation day, or even fire them. Jim, who worked in a food packing plant, described how he would often be told at 3:00 p.m. that he needed to stay late at work, even though he was due to pick up his daughter at day care by 4:30 p.m. This would require a series of phone calls to his wife or parents, who all worked as well, to see if someone could pick up the baby. "It is just hard to balance schedules because you can't plan for it."

I headed into this project fully prepared to hear stories of heartless workplace policies and rigid supervisors. The narrative about low-wage jobs with which we are most familiar is that they are inflexible, unsupportive, and monotonous. I was less prepared to hear uplifting stories, in which mothers and fathers felt supported at their jobs and grateful for the flexibility and leave time they were provided. Shonda, a customer service worker at a shipping company, often helped with managing packages in the stockroom, a task that became more challenging in the later months of pregnancy. She described her boss and coworkers as being completely supportive. "They've been really good to me. Once I told them that I was pregnant, they made sure I wasn't lifting things. When it started to get towards the end, and I was more tired and more swollen [laughs], they made sure I had a stool, which isn't policy. I mean, you're not allowed to sit down and ring or sit down at the registers, but they made sure I had a stool." Shonda's story reveals, somewhat surprisingly, that quite minor gestures can make some workers feel meaningfully supported.

Jarrod, a maintenance worker at a large health-care company, felt like he had hit the jackpot with his new job. "I have to say, this company is the third-biggest company I've worked for, and they are the best I've ever seen or even heard of, as far as you know, being responsive to your family's needs. You know, with the personal time they give you and flextime. They have day care on-site. They really, if you have any kind of family concern, they're very receptive to honoring any request you have." I asked Jarrod if he was happy with the child care. "Oh no, we don't use it . . . way too expensive."

These stories highlight the way that workplace policies shape mothers' and fathers' experiences of parenthood in both dramatic and everyday ways. Not being able to stay at the hospital with your premature baby is a nightmare that no parent should be forced to endure. But these tragic examples were rare. More often, it was the everyday inconveniences, like not being allowed to sit at the register during your third trimester of pregnancy, or being required to work an overtime shift when you are scheduled to pick up your baby from day care, that created chronic and overwhelming stress. In some cases, as Jarrod and Shonda noted, a few good workplace policies, whether formal or informal, made a world of difference.

## The Importance of the First Year of Parenthood

As a society, we have paid much attention to the first transition new parents face, that of having an infant. Shelves are stocked with volumes for new parents, offering advice on how to manage everything from breast-feeding, to sleep training, to clipping tiny fingernails. Yet we have woefully underestimated the impact of the second transition—that of returning to paid work very soon after birth—on both parents' and children's well-being. Our society offers new parents virtually no advice about how to manage the return to work during a time when many are still struggling to get out of their pajamas before noon. In fact, the majority of studies and advice books on the transition to parenthood simply never mention the physical, emotional, and logistical challenges of returning to one's job.

As noted previously, in the United States the only federal legislation covering parental leave is the Family and Medical Leave Act (FMLA) of 1993.[7] The FMLA provides up to twelve weeks of unpaid, job-protected medical or family leave to eligible workers. To be "eligible" an employee must work for a private sector employer with at least fifty employees, a public agency, or a school. In addition, the employee must have worked for the employer for at least 1,250 hours during the prior twelve months. As a result of these requirements, roughly 40 percent of workers are ineligible for unpaid leave, and the proportion of low-wage workers who are ineligible is significantly higher, since they often have not been employed long enough with one employer or worked enough hours in the previous year to qualify.

Because many low-income parents cannot afford to live without three months of wages, even the majority of those who qualify for unpaid leave return to work well before they are physically or emotionally ready. As we saw, again and again, mothers in our study headed back to work just a few weeks after birth because they simply could not afford to stay home. Of those who took the full twelve weeks of unpaid leave, over 70 percent reported high financial stress as a result of the lost income. As for paid leave, the disparity between high-wage and low-wage workers is even more significant. According to a 2014 White House report, high-wage workers in professional occupations are twice as likely to have paid parental leave than low-wage workers.[8]

So how did parents manage the logistics of returning to work after the birth of their child? What policies did they have available to them? What supports actually helped? First, we learned that parents were often emotionally unprepared for the first time they had to leave their infant to go back to paid work. As they described that first week back on the job, both mothers and fathers were emotional, swinging from tears to laughter, almost as if they were still shell-shocked. They said things like "I felt like I was losing an arm when I dropped her off at the sitters" and "I had no idea how hard it was going to be to leave him with a stranger."

Our quantitative data reflected this parental angst as shown in figure 2. This graph shows that mothers' depressive symptoms peak right before the birth. Our measure of depression assessed emotional feelings like "I felt sad" or "I could not get going," but also physical symptoms like trouble sleeping or a poor appetite. The inclusion of these physical indicators explains, in part, why mothers' scores were so high around the birth. After the birth, mothers' depressive symptoms dropped sharply, a pattern that has been documented in much of the literature on postpartum mental health. What was new and surprising in our data was the upward trend that appeared after mothers returned to work. This finding is critical because it shows that within three months of returning to paid work, new mothers are at increased risk for depression.

Turning to fathers, we saw no changes in their reports of depressive symptoms across the first year of parenthood. However, we did see changes in their feelings of anxiety. Similar to the pattern displayed by mothers' depression, fathers' anxiety peaked at the time of the birth, significantly declined after the

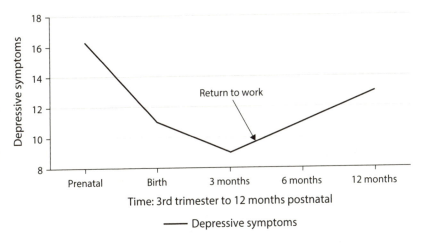

FIGURE 2. Change in mothers' depressive symptoms across transition to parenthood.

birth, and increased again when mothers returned to work. Why did we see changes in mothers' depression but fathers' anxiety (not their depression)? One possibility is that fathers may be more comfortable reporting symptoms of anxiety ("I am restless" or "I couldn't calm down") as opposed to the more emotional assessments of depression ("I am sad" or "I feel depressed"). The most important point from these results is that both mothers and fathers experience changing emotions across these multiple transitions.

If we left the story here, then the simple conclusion would be that an early return to low-wage work is related to poorer mental health for new parents. However, average trajectories tell us little about the ways in which individual mothers and fathers coped after birth. From our interviews, we knew that some parents were coping very well with their new roles, while others were struggling. This variability is dramatically illustrated in figure 3, which charts the depression trajectories of

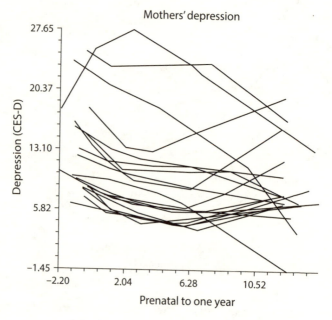

FIGURE 3. Individual differences in change in mothers' depressive symptoms across the transition to parenthood.

twenty randomly chosen mothers from the prenatal interview to one year postpartum. As the set of lines shows, there are dramatic differences in how mothers' mental health changed across the year. Some mothers reported few depressive symptoms across the first year, some reported high symptoms across the year, and others experienced decreases and increases over time. The same was true for fathers, especially with respect to anxiety.

Why do some low-income, working parents maintain good mental health while others do not? The availability of formal and informal workplace policies—such as parental leave, flexibility, and child-care supports—explains some of the variation. Research from other countries demonstrates that paid parental leave gives new mothers time to recover, work out a feeding schedule, and sleep, all factors that positively affect maternal well-being. Similarly, once back at work, some schedule flexibility and feeling comfortable with child care are important ingredients for parental well-being. A recent report issued by the National Women's Law Center (NWLC) summed up the situation well:

> For many low-wage, working parents, the conditions of their jobs effectively set them up to fail: meeting both their work and family obligations becomes an impossible juggling act. Parents report that they are getting by on less sleep and don't have the time or resources to meet their own health needs. . . . Other features of low-wage work that increase parents' stress—including nonstandard and constantly fluctuating work hours, rigid attendance policies and a lack of any paid time off—can adversely affect children's development.[9]

The NWLC report highlights the findings from significant research that link conditions of parents' work to the developmental outcomes of the next generation. However, much remains to be learned about how formal and informal workplace policies distinguish low-income, working families who fare well during this time from those who flounder. We often adopt narratives that characterize all low-wage workers and their families as cut from the same cloth—facing the same challenges, which result in the same dire outcomes. As our data show, however, this is a mistake. There are times when employers fire workers for being pregnant or refuse to allow mothers any leave time after birth, but we also saw employers who offered to babysit or who paid mothers while they were on leave. What are the implications of these different experiences for new parents' well-being?

It is important to emphasize at the outset that among the families we interviewed, formal workplace policies, such as paid leave or on-site child care, were quite rare. Too often, workplace benefits depended on the kindness of supervisors, a topic we examine in the next chapter. At the same time, the policies that did exist "on the books," although quite meager, turned out to matter a great deal for some parents.

## How Much Parental Leave Did Parents Have?

The greatest challenge facing families was the lack of paid parental leave. When we asked parents how much parental leave their job provided, and if it was paid, the answers we were given were more complicated than we'd expected. For example, Delila, a home health aide, took a total of ten weeks off after the birth of her child. She cobbled together several different kinds of leave to do so. "I only had ten weeks off when Aidan was born. I used up ten vacation days, four sick days, and I had three comp days coming, so in all seventeen days of my leave was covered. The other thirty-three days were unpaid, and that hurt."

The type of patchwork leave that Delila described was the norm, not the exception. Parents used every possible benefit available to them to squeeze out a paid leave after the birth. The majority of parents used up the entire balance of their sick time, personal time, comp time, and vacation time to cover their leave, as they simply could not afford unpaid time off. This practice, however, created an unforeseen problem when parents returned to work. Once parents were back at work, it did not take long before their infants became ill, often the result of being exposed to other children at day care. Since parents had exhausted their paid benefits for their leave, they were left with few options to care for their children. They usually resorted to taking unearned time off, but doing so often resulted in penalties and sanctions at work. Cheryl, a fast food worker, received

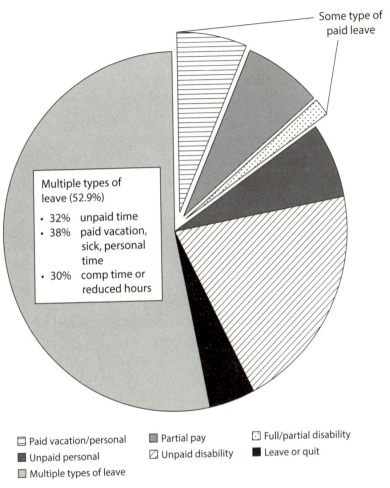

Some type of paid leave

Multiple types of leave (52.9%)
- 32%  unpaid time
- 38%  paid vacation, sick, personal time
- 30%  comp time or reduced hours

☐ Paid vacation/personal   ■ Partial pay   ⊡ Full/partial disability
■ Unpaid personal   ☑ Unpaid disability   ■ Leave or quit
☐ Multiple types of leave

FIGURE 4. Types of parental leaves used by mothers.
Note: Percent of mothers using different types of parental leave across the transition to parenthood.
Source: Perry-Jenkins, M., Smith, J. Z., Wadsworth, L. P., & Halpern, H. P. (2017). "Workplace Policies and Mental Health among Working-Class, New Parents." Community, Work and Family, 20(2), 226–249. https://doi-org.silk.library.umass .edu/10.1080/13668803.2016.1252721.

a written warning at work when she had to miss work to care for her infant daughter. "So, of course, the minute I started up my job again, she [the baby] got sick. She is around all these kids with runny noses, and they are touching her and stuff. Then I can't bring her to day care. I call my boss and say she is sick, I got to stay home. . . . He says you got no time. What am I supposed to do? I stayed home and got written up at work."

Our data show that pulling together a parental leave is messy and complicated. As shown in the large, left-side section of the pie chart in figure 4, slightly more than half of mothers, whether married, cohabiting, or single, used multiple types of paid and unpaid benefits to cover their leave. It turns out, unsurprisingly, that married or cohabiting families face fewer challenges than single mothers.

About a third of married mothers and almost half of single and cohabiting mothers received no income during their leave. Those who received pay relied primarily on disability benefits, along with their own personal, vacation, and sick time. Every family in our study who relied entirely on unpaid leave reported significant financial stress during this time, which they managed by drawing down savings, cutting expenses, relying on a partner's income, increasing credit card debt, receiving help from other family members, or combinations of these.

Nearly 20 percent of mothers simply quit their jobs when their baby was born, with the hope of finding a new job or being rehired when they were ready to go back to work. As one mother explained, it didn't really matter if she was working at Walmart or Target, and it was easier to quit than to deal with "supervisors breathing down your neck." For about half of the mothers, this strategy worked as they had hoped, and they found a new job, usually within weeks, when they were ready to return to work; the other half found themselves relying on family, friends, and Temporary Aid for Needy Families (TANF), a government program that assists families with children when they are unable to provide basic needs.

For the majority of mothers, access to parental leave was provided at the discretion of their supervisors. Some mothers reported that supervisors had little information about either federal parental leave policies or the policies within their own state or company. One supervisor told an expectant mother that she was not allowed to use her earned vacation time after the baby was born because that was not what vacation time was intended to cover, but she could use her sick time. In other cases, the mothers were unaware of the FMLA policy and found themselves requesting "time off" with little or no knowledge of their rights or pertinent federal regulations.

For fathers, there was virtually no discussion about taking time off after the birth, with either partners or employers. Both mothers and fathers had few, if any, expectations that fathers would stay home and share parenting duties during those first early weeks of parenthood. On average, fathers took five days leave, with most taking just three. This leave was covered primarily by using vacation time or, in a few cases, sick days, if their employer allowed them to do so. Even in cases where parents were aware of the FMLA and knew that fathers had access to it, fathers did not take any unpaid leave time after the birth. Research from European countries that provide paid leave for both mothers and fathers shows that fathers in these countries are also less likely to use this benefit.[10] Often, stigma stands in the way of fathers taking leave, as many fathers fear that they will be seen as less serious workers if they take parental leave. Recently, a number of Scandinavian countries and Canada have modified their leave policies to provide some paid leave that is available only to fathers; it is not transferable to mothers, and if fathers do not use it, they forfeit the time. This change has resulted in fathers taking longer leaves. These findings are important to keep in mind as a number of states in the United States begin to offer paid leave to new parents.

## Was Parental Leave Related to Parents' Mental Health?

Research on the effects of leave on maternal mental health has primarily been conducted outside of the United States. Given the ubiquity of short, unpaid leaves in the United States, there is very little variability in length of leave time to examine, especially for low-wage workers. It should be noted, in the short time between the collection of our data in the mid-2000s and 2021, nine states in the United States have begun to institute paid leave policies, creating opportunities for natural experiments to test the effects on parents and employers. Massachusetts instituted paid leave policy on January 1, 2021—too late for the families in this study but a great step forward for future families.

Data from European studies show that longer paid leaves predict better health outcomes for infants and better mental and physical health outcomes for mothers. One reason for this is that when mothers have access to paid leave, they nurse longer, which is linked to numerous health benefits for infants and better mental health outcomes for mothers. Based on this evidence, we thought that longer leaves for the mothers in our study would be related to better mental health. To our surprise, the results were not that straightforward. Length of leave, whether paid or unpaid, was unrelated to the mental health of married mothers. It did, however, have a positive effect for single and cohabiting mothers.[11]

Why were some of our results (those for married mothers) different from the findings of the European studies mentioned above? It appears that the answer is primarily that the terms "long leave" and "short leave" have significantly different meanings in the United States and abroad. In the international studies that found positive effects of "longer" parental leaves on mothers' well-being, a "long leave" was defined as a leave lasting at least six months, and often included leaves lasting up to a year. In these studies, a leave that lasted twelve weeks was considered a "short leave." Thus, a "short leave" in these studies was actually on the longer side for the mothers in our study. Among our mothers, only three took more than six months of leave. Given the short leaves offered to US mothers, as well as the minimal variability in the length of their leaves, it is not surprising that maternity leave did not have a positive impact for married mothers.

For fathers, however, we found that when mothers took longer leaves (meaning more than six weeks), fathers' anxiety declined across the first year of parenthood. When mothers had more time at home after the birth, fathers slept more, had fewer family responsibilities, and more easily managed work and family duties. It is puzzling that the positive effects of a longer maternal leave lasted throughout the first year of parenthood for fathers, even after mothers were back at work. It appears that the early patterns established during the leave, where mothers usually take on more family work, persisted even upon mothers' return to work, which buffered fathers from stress and anxiety.

Unlike married mothers, single and cohabiting mothers did realize better mental health from longer leaves. Longer parental leaves, again contrasting short leaves (two to three weeks) with long leaves (twelve weeks), were related to less depression one year out and faster declines in depression. Why the difference from the experiences of married mothers? It may simply be that parental leave is more protective for families who face greater financial and family challenges, which was more often the case for single and cohabiting mothers. This would be consistent with other research, which shows that the low-income parents most likely to benefit from supportive interventions are those who are worst off.

Parents' stories frequently highlighted the stress caused by short and unpaid leaves. Many mothers spoke about not being fully recovered from the birth physically, and mothers and fathers regularly talked about the struggles of managing sleep routines, as well as the emotional toll of leaving their child with someone else at such a young age. Carrie was a direct care service worker who was trying to figure out how to extend her leave. As she shared, "We didn't plan to conceive. She was kind of a surprise, and Gary had a little bit more difficulty accepting it, whereas I believe in the theory that everything happens for a reason, and so you know she's coming for a reason, and that's that, and he was a little scared. But he's come around, and we are very excited but nervous. Our finances are less [laughs] than we would like them to be, so it makes things a little bit more stressful. Especially my job only pays five days maternity leave, so we're trying to figure out how we can stretch that to eight weeks, if not twelve, because I can't imagine going back after five days. I have a strenuous job. I have to lift people and care for them, so I can't even imagine." As it turned out, Carrie was able to take six weeks paid leave because her employer let her use her "future" vacation and sick time.

Becky, who worked in a sales office, highlighted the emotional dimension of becoming a new parent without any recognition of that fact at work. "I happen to have a good boss, and him and I have a good relationship. But other than that, it [the company] is not supportive at all. I mean, two weeks after my coming back from my maternity leave, they were trying to send me away for a week. And I'm like, 'I can't leave a three-month-old newborn alone for a week, you psychos!' [laughs] I was like, 'You can't do that!' And they're like, 'Well, that's what the job entails,' and they're just like, 'Well, that's how it's going to be, or you have to leave!' They don't offer any type of part-time kind of thing, they don't offer any type of day-care assistance, they don't offer any type of personal-family leave time. Like I've actually used up all of my vacation days having to call in because something's happened with the baby." Although Becky scored very low on our depression scale, she was extremely stressed and felt she had "too much to do and not enough time to do it." Although we did not assess parents' anger—we should have—it was clear to me that Becky, like many parents, was extremely angry.

Short parental leaves prevented parents from setting up routines around sleep, feedings, and baths. Many parents in our study were subsisting on far less sleep than they needed, especially in cases in which their infant had colic or other health issues. Recent research shows that most new parents, mothers in particular, function with severe sleep deprivation for the first six to twelve months after their child is born. Sleep deprivation negatively affects parents' ability to function during the daytime, as well as their general well-being.[12] It also puts parents at risk for postpartum depression.[13] The fact that most parents in the United States return to work so soon after birth results in many parents performing their job duties under extreme duress. In certain low-wage jobs, the risk to health and safety imposed by sleep deprivation is a serious concern. Tyrone, a new dad who reported getting about three to four hours of sleep each night because his baby girl "had her nights and days mixed up," described literally falling asleep at work—he worked in a sheet metal shop.

When mothers returned to work, they often decided to stop breast-feeding because the logistics were simply too difficult. Many mothers even preemptively stopped. Robin, who worked at a bank, had begun to nurse right after the birth but quickly decided to stop because she knew she had to return to work in six weeks. "I just decided. . . . We went to the breast-feeding class, and we talked about it and stuff, and I was thinking I was going to, and then I just decided to bottle-feed because I was going to go back to work soon anyway. I didn't want to have to pump my milk and stuff. I did end up, like a week after I had her, trying to breast-feed, but it didn't go very well, so I went back to the bottle." Robin's thinking reflected that of many mothers, who thought it was too much trouble to start nursing, since it was going to be virtually impossible to do so once they went back to work. As mothers described their challenges with nursing, there was often a sense of relief in making the decision to stop, rather than sadness or remorse. As Taylor described, "I get my body back, he can help feed her, and I don't have to pump . . . win, win, win."

One significant challenge to maintaining breast-feeding practices upon returning to work is that few work sites, especially in low-wage occupations, provide the private space or the time for mothers to pump their milk. Angel was employed as a guard in a prison; not only were there no locked doors, but her coworkers were almost all men, and she felt uncomfortable about asking for a space to pump. "They're not very sensitive to individual needs, I would say. You know, like I said, there's no privacy to go anywhere and pump the milk or anything like that. But I think they try to be flexible as far as if you need time off for anything, appointments or if the kids are sick. I think they try. . . . It's just that whole milk thing. [laughs] That's my biggest grudge because on top of not having the milk for her and having to supplement with formula, my body is still producing the milk, which causes discomfort for me, which is a pain."

Becoming a nursing mother is a challenging experience for many women. Engorged breasts, cracked nipples, dehydration, and exhaustion are some of the early hurdles new mothers need to overcome before they feel skilled at breast-feeding; the mothers we interviewed were no exception. Couple these challenges with the fact that, prior to the Affordable Care Act of 2010,[14] there were virtually no protections for employed mothers to pump milk at work, and no private places to pump, and it is no wonder that breast-feeding drops off so quickly. The majority of mothers in this study had no designated sites at work to pump milk, and few had scheduled breaks that gave them time to pump. Not surprisingly, while 73 percent of mothers reported at the prenatal interview that they planned to nurse, only 29 percent were nursing one month after birth, and only 17 percent of mothers were nursing at three months.

The significant decline in breast-feeding rates that our mothers reported flies in the face of public health goals in the United States. The Department of Health and Human Services, for example, recommends that mothers exclusively breast-feed for the first six months of the baby's life because of the health benefits for both mother and infant.[15] We know, moreover, that women from lower social classes are less likely to breast-feed than their more advantaged counterparts.[16] Women with less than a high school education, for instance, are far less likely to breast-feed than women who have received a college degree.[17] The workplace is an important site where these social class differences play out. Women employed in low-wage jobs, with short leaves and little flexibility, simply don't have the adequate time and supports to maintain breast-feeding. Many mothers in our study felt great tension between the recommendations to nurse from their OB/GYNs and pediatricians, and the reality of breast-feeding demands in everyday life. Breast-feeding was simply not sustainable for most.

## Schedule Flexibility

Once parents returned to paid work, issues related to schedule flexibility and control over work hours became paramount. Ina, who worked in the stockroom at large box store, was surprised by the challenges she faced when she returned to work ten weeks after her daughter Samantha was born. For example, restrictive personal and sick time policies quickly became a problem. As she shared, "Well, we have five times to be absent for whatever reason . . . regardless of the excuses, and then your job is threatened. It didn't matter if your baby was sick, or your babysitter canceled. I got up to four unexcused absences and then could not handle the stress." Ina quit and looked for a new job. At a time when parents are most in need of flexibility, low-wage hourly jobs are the least likely to offer that support. Although many companies have policies that provide limited allowances for planned time off, such as for a doctor's appointment, these absences must be planned days or weeks in advance. Few companies have policies that provide for the last-minute illnesses and scheduling conflicts that commonly arise for new parents.

I was interested in understanding what types of scheduling flexibility parents had in their jobs and whether scheduling flexibility had an impact on their mental health. There are two distinct types of flexibility. First, there are formal policies, such as flextime, where an employee has core hours during which they need to be at work but are free to alter their start and stop times. Other formal policies allowed parents to take time off for a child's doctor appointment without being required to make up the hours. Very few of the workers in our study had access to formal flextime policies. Second, and in contrast, informal policies, often required for last-minute or emergency situations like needing to leave early to care for an ill child or come in late because of a child-care problem, were more common but varied significantly between jobs.

We asked parents about a number of different policies and benefits that a company might offer, like paid sick time or the option to work a four-day workweek. Parents first reported on whether their company had the policy and then whether they had ever used the policy or benefit. The most commonly reported policy available to mothers and fathers was "flexibility in daily work schedule." We asked about this as a "formal policy" but found out that in over 80 percent of the cases, this was actually an informal arrangement. About half of new mothers and slightly fewer fathers could take time off for doctor appointments or child-care emergencies with short notice. Our data also showed that if a parent had access to this kind of schedule flexibility, he or she tended to use it.

A majority of new parents reported that their company offered paid personal and sick days, but only about half of these parents actually took advantage of this benefit. Given their demanding family responsibilities, I was surprised that so many parents were not using this benefit when available. After some scrutiny of the data, a couple of reasons emerged to explain this finding. First, some of the parents had not been at their companies long enough to access these benefits. Second, others reported that they had access only to personal days, rather than to sick days, and that personal days had to be scheduled ahead of time. If you tried to call in to use a personal day when you or your child was sick, you could be (and often were) denied the day off.

In our interviews, we heard mixed assessments of how scheduling policies supported new parents. We asked parents: Can you provide any specific examples of supportive policies that your company has to help you deal with your family responsibilities? Robert, who worked as a floor installer, mentioned a new policy that had recently been enacted in Massachusetts called the Small Necessities Leave Act.[18] "They just allot you, I think it's sixteen hours per year for taking off for like bringing your child to the hospital for an exam or getting shots or something like that, or taking any family member. They can't, as long as you give them notice, they can't deny you the time." In contrast, some parents experienced an utter lack of control over when they worked. Avery, a data entry employee at the state hospital, described her scheduling as quite rigid. "There isn't any arrangement besides my regular job schedule. If I need a day off, if I need time off, I would request it ahead of time. And if it was a last-minute thing, I would have to speak with her, speak with my supervisor as soon as I could and maybe set up something if it was possible. If it's not possible, then it just can't happen. It's not like I'm slaving over there, but it's only flexible to an extent. There are not that many options with their options." When I asked how she coped with an unexpected illness she told me, "It's just better if I know what I need in advance because the last-minute stuff with last-minute and unplanned tardies, unplanned absences, you don't get much of those before they let you go. They work like this: five is a verbal warning, six is written, and seven is termination. So . . . there you go."

A number of parents talked about the pressure to stay late at work to complete tasks and meet a deadline, a significant problem if, for example, they needed to pick up their baby at day care. As Charl, a worker at a delivery company, described, "Sometimes you don't get out at your scheduled time. If it's real busy, they don't let you out right away. And that can be a problem, especially if you have a day care that's just waiting and waiting."

## Is Scheduling Flexibility Related to Parents' Well-Being?

Although scheduling flexibility was quite limited, overall, some mothers and fathers reported having good flexibility at work. How did this difference relate to new parents' mental health? As it turned out, the existence of even minimal scheduling flexibility had a positive impact on working mothers. Mothers who reported having some flexibility at work had better mental health than those reporting little flexibility. Importantly, it was *having* the policy, not necessarily using it, that produced positive outcomes. Simply knowing one can leave, if necessary, may make work less stressful and contribute to better morale and health. It may also be that the availability of a benefit, even if you have not used it yet, is an indication of a workplace that is more supportive of work-family balance and that this general support is associated with good health.

For new mothers, having both longer parental leaves (twelve weeks) and scheduling flexibility turned out to be a powerful combination. As figure 5 shows, mothers who had both longer leaves and better scheduling polices (represented by the dotted line at bottom) had lower levels of depression across the first year of parenthood than mothers with short leaves and little flexibility (represented by the dark solid line at top). What is most compelling about these findings is that we are not talking about large accommodations; simply having a slightly longer

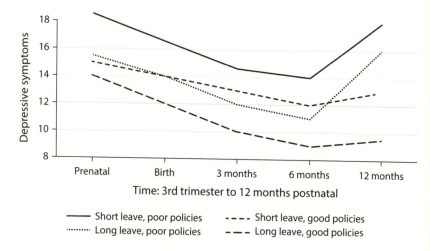

FIGURE 5. Length of leave, supportive policies, and new mothers'
depressive symptoms.

leave and some minimal scheduling flexibility, like being able
to leave work for a doctor's appointment, had positive implications for new mothers' mental health.

Although depression among new mothers has been the subject of significant study and intervention efforts for decades, few
have considered the workplace as a potential site for intervention. A reasonable conclusion from our findings is that providing mothers with three months of leave and some scheduling
flexibility upon return to work after birth can provide significant protection for mothers' mental health.

Although we saw that schedule flexibility helped new
mothers, it did not seem to matter for fathers, at least in terms
of their mental health. Since mothers more often shouldered
the lion's share of family responsibilities, it may be that fathers
did not feel the need for more flexibility. Mothers, for instance,
consistently reported more tension over negotiating time off to
take children to doctor appointments or arrange care for an ill

child. Nevertheless, fathers did have strong opinions about the need for job flexibility. Randy, a printing machine operator, addressed the opaque nature of the policies at his workplace: "Uh, well, the policies are very few and far between. Whatever they even are, you don't really know. It's a gray area until you ask or something happens, then you got to try and find out. And with the supervisors, they don't find out, all they think about is themselves." Jamal, who worked as a custodian at a large factory, described strict rules around flexibility. "Oh yeah, they're getting a lot stricter on a lot of the policies. Tardiness, lunch breaks, working increased hours. Being maintenance, pretty much it has always been like, 'Well, this thing broke. We need you in,' and . . . I always need to drop what I am doing to go in. I don't know that I would ever actually get in trouble for it. But, I do know that they'd be pretty pissed off, and I'd probably get a good chewing out on Monday if I said, 'No, I'm not working on Sunday, 'cause I need the time off.'"

On the other hand, some company policies, or at least supervisors' interpretation of those policies, were quite supportive. As Chance, who worked as a mechanic, described, "Our department is very responsive. They bend over backwards to do anything for you and your family. My grandmother passed away. Company policy is eight hours paid for funeral/wake; my department said take as long as you need. Also, when we got married, I had just started there. They let me take ten days no problem."

Every company had some sort of policies regarding schedule flexibility, be it paid or unpaid, planned or last minute. But quite often it was the supervisors who had the final say in how those policies were carried out. In the next chapter we explore in greater detail the influence of supervisors on the job experiences of new parents.

## Child-Care Benefits

Beyond leave time and flexibility, the other main workplace policy we discussed with parents was child care. Parents were stressed about how to find child care, how to afford it, and, most importantly, how safe and good it was. Most expressed extreme ambivalence about using child care, saying things like "She may not remember I am her mother," or "I worry that they won't take care of her like I would."

Few companies offer child-care supports, and for low-income workers, child-care supports are virtually nonexistent. Barriers to finding high-quality child care for low-income, working parents are numerous. First, the average costs of full-time infant care in Massachusetts is $17,062 a year, or $1,422 a month.[19] This means that for "average" child care, parents earning close to minimum wage would need to use anywhere from 50 percent to 80 percent of their income to cover this single expense. In addition, the fact that many low-income workers have variable work schedules, work nonstandard shifts, and often receive their work schedules only days before the next workweek makes finding reliable child-care arrangements nearly impossible.

About 30 percent of the couples in our study managed child-care challenges by working opposite shifts. For example, one parent would work 7 a.m. to 3 p.m., while the other worked 3 p.m. to 11 p.m. Often, schedules were so tight that couples devised creative ways to manage the child-care handoff. For example, Jessie worked the 7:00 to 3:00 shift at a local paper factory, and her husband, Ivan, started his job as a security guard at 3:00 p.m. Jessie received permission from her boss to work through her lunch break and leave work at 2:30, in order to meet Ivan at a rest stop on the highway. The "Emma handoff," as they called it, involved a quick exchange. Ivan would provide an update on Emma's day, including eating, napping, and diaper changes; there was a kiss good-bye; and both were on their way.

Although this strategy dramatically reduced the cost of care and eased many parents' concerns about delegating caregiving to a stranger, the costs in terms of parents' mental health and relationships were high. We found that mothers who worked evening shifts (e.g., 3 p.m. to 11 p.m.) had higher levels of depression than mothers on day shifts. Families in which mothers worked rotating shifts, meaning her hours varied every few weeks between day and evening shifts, reported the highest levels of couple conflict; this result is unsurprising, since rotating one's work hours every few weeks makes it virtually impossible to maintain a consistent family routine. Fathers who worked evening and night shifts also reported more depressive symptoms than fathers working day shifts.[20]

Child-care benefits were virtually unheard of for most parents in our study. We asked parents about whether they had access to numerous types of child-care benefits, such as child-care referral services, dependent care assistance plans, or on-site child care. The percentage of parents having any one of these child-care benefits was never more than 25 percent, and even in cases where they had access to a benefit, only a small percentage of parents used the benefit. For example, a dependent care assistance plan (DCAP), which is a benefit that allows parents to take pretax dollars out of their pay to cover child-care costs, can save parents up to 20 percent of their costs. Twenty-five percent of mothers had a DCAP plan at work; but only about half of them used the benefit. When we asked them why they didn't use a benefit that could save them a considerable amount of money, it was clear some had been advised not to. One mother said that when she talked to Human Resources about the DCAP, she was told that it was very complicated and that she could lose money if she overestimated her child-care costs. Another mother was told that it would save her only a few hundred dollars each year and wasn't worth the paperwork. In short, HR at several companies, instead of helping employees' access benefits, discouraged their use of the DCAP.

Although parents had very limited child-care benefits, we still examined whether having any child-care supports at all was related to parents' mental health. To our surprise, fathers who reported having at least one child-care benefit, like some type of referral system or subsidized benefits, reported less anxiety. It may be that workplaces that offer any recognition or support for the birth of a child ease new fathers' anxiety. Moreover, given how few companies offer child-care supports in the United States, companies offering even minimal benefits may also just be better companies to work for in a variety of ways. Since some of our fathers did not even tell their supervisors that they had become a new parent, it may be that when a company does acknowledge that male workers could be fathers and need support, it is perceived as supportive by fathers. For mothers, we did not see the same positive effect; we suspect this is because supports were not only rare, but minimal when they existed.

The majority of families used some type of family day-care arrangements for their infants or, when it was available, relative care. Parents often expressed extreme distrust of child-care centers. Kelly, who worked in housekeeping at a large hotel, stated emphatically, "Those places [child-care centers] are not good for kids. They don't care about your baby, and they rob you blind." Kendra, who worked in data entry at a local health-care company, returned to work four weeks after her baby was born. Within the first few months of being back at the job, Kendra had already missed a number of days of work because either her child or her child-care provider was ill. Her supervisor confronted her. "She said that some people have trouble handling the job, and once they get the job, they realize they can't handle it. So I had to convince her that that wasn't the situation, and it just so happened my kid was sick because of day care. They weren't used to day care, and the day care provider was sick, and it was really tough in the beginning. So they thought that I couldn't handle it. That's the perfect example of work making it difficult."

When we asked fathers about child-care supports, they often discussed their own logistical challenges arranging care and their feelings about using child care, rarely discussing policies or benefits that could help. Sean described the angst of leaving his baby each day with a sitter: "We both go to work, I drop her off in the morning, she picks her up at night. It is hard to drop her off in general 'cause you know, leaving your baby with somebody, is kind of like uch! But she has been good. We lucked out with the babysitter." Few parents held expectations that their workplaces would offer support for child care. A number of fathers mentioned that having child care at work would be great but often dismissed the idea immediately as beyond the realm of possibility. Dan, a young father of twenty-three who worked as a cook, noted, "It'd be nice if the workplace provided day care and offered part-time hours; that would be nice, but they don't. We've looked into other positions for Raquel [his wife] and the possibility of her staying home, but . . . not really possible." Joe, who worked in a gun factory, noted, "The policies are pretty much OK. They could be better, but they're still working on the child-care issue, and it has been put on the back burner unfortunately. Our other plant has child care, and there's a lot of like new babies coming into the factory, new parents, so everybody's got the same issue. Yeah, child care would be cool." When we asked Alan, a maintenance worker, if he had any ideas about what policies might help him and his wife cope, he responded, "Have I thought of anything? Um, other than maybe a day-care center on-site, ha ha [the subtext being that that will never happen]. . . . Other than that, that's about all that could change to make it better."

Fears about child-care arrangements were common but came up only after we had interviewed families multiple times. It was usually not until parents switched child-care providers that they would tell us what they didn't like about a former provider. Parents found it extremely difficult to admit when they were unhappy with their current child-care arrangements, and often parents kept their children in settings with which they were not satisfied because they simply had no other options. But once they switched arrangements, we heard about concerns, like the high number of children being cared for, naps that seemed to last too long, and unexplained bumps and bruises. Joe was concerned about the attention and care his daughter was getting, and her exposure to the older children in the family day care: "Well, just that she is not going to get the full attention she needs 'cause of the other kids being around. We don't want her just stuck in a corner somewhere while she's [the provider is] feeding the other kids. They [the kids] are not getting the total attention they need, so that's a concern, but it's a minor concern 'cause she does as good as she can possibly do. . . . Certain things might be unsafe for them, with older kids around, so that's a concern. But like I said, she does a good job of keeping them separate, and if they're with the other kids, she's watching them. She doesn't leave them unattended with the other kids. So that's good."

There were also positive stories. Bud was very happy with the family day care they used for their daughter. "I am very satisfied. It's worked out well. She takes real good care of the kids. She has like little parties for them on their birthdays and on holidays.

For caring, including my kid, she probably has eight kids there at times, and she looks after them really nice. She has a separate room for the babies, where they can sleep, she keeps them in a separate room, and brings them out some of the time so she can, so they can integrate, but she's taken care of them really well, from what I've seen."

Finally, a number of parents had full or partial child-care support provided by family members. This came with costs as well as benefits. As Ashley, who worked as an elder-care assistant, described her situation, "Well my mother and father take him on Monday and Wednesday, and my mother-in-law has him on Tuesday and Thursday, which is kind of great. Don't get me wrong, I am thankful, but they really have different styles. My mom is all about routine, routine, routine, and my mother-in-law is way more laid back . . . and me, I am somewhere in the middle. It is a little stressful but what can I say . . . it is free." Lucia, conversely, ranted for fifteen minutes about how hard it was to have your own mother help care for your baby. "She is all preachy and know-it-ally, and she acts like I don't know my own baby. She thinks it is her baby, and it isn't. Plus, my mother gets her during her good time, in the morning and early day, and I come home to a tired, cranky baby. Just does not feel fair." Inevitably, it seemed, even though infants were getting loving care at no expense, grandparent care came with nonmonetary costs for new parents.

## For Low-Income New Parents, Even Small Policies and Benefits Matter

The new moms and dads with whom we spoke confirmed what much of the research says: low-income workers have little in the way of workplace supports, such as parental leave or schedule flexibility, that could help them manage the demands of new parenthood. Although the majority of parents had access to some amount of parental leave (usually unpaid), the costs of using unpaid leave meant most returned to work well before they exhausted this benefit. We heard stories of unsupportive, rigid supervisors who refused to comply with policies at all, but also of supervisors who said, "Take what you need, we will be here when you are ready." In terms of schedule flexibility, some supervisors almost refused to acknowledge a birth had occurred. As Maya shared, "I walked into work on my first day back, and my supervisor didn't even acknowledge that anything was different. He told me to get started with merchandise in aisle 11." Other supervisors bent over backward to help parents be parents. Finally, child care was challenging for everyone, but not necessarily for the same reason. For some, it was the costs; for others, the quality; and for yet others, the stress of parenting with one's own parent.

Many parents were not prepared to negotiate leave time, flexibility, or even child-care issues with their supervisors. Most of the parents were young, had little experience in the working world, and did not know how to make requests of a boss or negotiate a day off when their child was ill. This was never clearer than with Rayon, a telemarketer who was nearing the end of her six-month probation period on the job. Once she reached six months on the job, she would start to receive benefits, including leave time and vacation. With three weeks remaining in her probationary period, her baby became ill with an ear infection. She was stuck. She had no back-up plan for child care. She also made no attempt to call her boss to ask for more time off; she simply stayed home with her baby. The next day, when she walked into work, she was fired on the spot. She was completely shocked. She begged her supervisor for another chance, but since she had violated policy before her probationary period was over, she was out. She called me that day in tears, wondering what to do next. She had no real options except to start looking for another job. I raise this example to note that the challenges facing new parents are complicated, and new parents often lack any road map to navigate this new terrain. Clearly, there is room for better policies and benefits, but I also think that better education and mentoring of young workers who become parents would ameliorate some of the problems that we witnessed.

This chapter started with the heartbreaking story of Lyla, a new mother who returned to work five days after giving birth to her premature child, so she could save her parental leave time for when her baby was released from the hospital. Months later, we learned that, as she had planned, Lyla was able to take her parental leave when her infant son came home. However, she did not have an easy time. Jaylen faced health challenges, as many premature infants do. He was colicky and had breathing problems. As Lyla began to search for child care, she realized that it was virtually impossible to find providers willing to care for a child with Jaylen's problems. Lyla, very reluctantly, moved in with her mother and did not return to work. When we last spoke, she was receiving Temporary Aid for Needy Families, something she had vowed she would never do during our first interview with her: "I would never take aid; I can make my own way." But a year later, Lyla was struggling. "This was not my plan. I love my son, but he is all I have. No friends, no work, no nothing." Had Lyla's scenario played out in another country somewhere in the world such as Canada or Sweden, she would have had a full year or more of paid leave to care for her infant. By the end of this period, he likely would have been stable enough for a child-care setting. Instead, she became one of the casualties of an inadequate and inhumane US system that fails to support families at their most vulnerable moments. These stories answer, at least in part, the question of why low-income children in the United States are not thriving in comparison with children in other nations: work policies, both formal and informal, matter for parents and children. It is that simple, and that straightforward.

# CHAPTER 4

# "They Treat Me Right, Then I Do Right by Them"

*Experiences in Low-Income Jobs and Mental Health*

After twenty harrowing minutes spent trying to climb Linda and Mac's steep, icy driveway in the middle of February, my graduate student and I were feeling a bit rattled by the time we reached the front door. Linda immediately put on the water for tea and laid out some cookies on the kitchen table. The couple lived in a classic, 1970s A-frame house with a large family room attached to the back and a wood-burning stove—quite lovely given the subzero temperatures outside. It was obvious that Linda was excited to talk to us, but Mac appeared to have been dragged into this interview somewhat begrudgingly. I settled down with Linda at the kitchen table, while my student and Mac went into the back room to talk. As I began the interview, Linda immediately declared, "I believe it is so important to have work-family balance, and so many people don't. I am sure we will get to this, but you should know I have it really good." Linda worked at a candle factory, where her job involved packing customer orders for eight hours each day. As far as good jobs go, hers would not have been at the top of my list; I was intrigued.

Is there such a thing as "good" low-wage work? In this chapter, I explore this question by looking more closely at the jobs held by low-income parents. What happens in these jobs? What does a typical day look like? To what extent do the workers enjoy the work? Over the past decade, reports from think tanks, academia, and even the federal government have documented the poor work conditions under which many Americans labor, which often include low wages, unpredictable work schedules, lack of paid sick or personal time, and little flexibility.[1][2][3] Important policy efforts are underway to address these workplace inequities, which, as the previous chapter demonstrated, negatively affect the well-being of low-income, working parents. However, our society's current focus on policies that give parents time away from work to care for their family often overlooks the fact that *parents spend much of their lives at work.* How do parents' experiences, day in and day out, on the factory floor or in the beauty salon, affect them and their families?

Contrary to popular narratives, some low-income jobs can be energizing, satisfying, and empowering. In such cases, work tends to enhance workers' overall well-being. The opposite is also true. When low-wage jobs are demoralizing, stressful, and mind-numbing, they tend to impose psychological harms that extend beyond the workplace. By looking at differences within workers' experiences in low-wage jobs, rather than comparing them to the experiences of the high-wage workers, our research was able to identify what about low-wage work is good and protective for workers, and what is detrimental.

I had many questions to ask Linda about why she felt that she "had it good" at work. "What do you actually do all day at work?" "What kind of relationship do you have with your supervisor?"

"What are coworker relationships like?" As Linda filled out our questionnaires and elaborated on her experiences, I noticed that her description of her job highlighted many key characteristics of any good job: some degree of control over your work, supportive supervisors, collegial coworkers, and opportunities for growth. How does a factory job provide such conditions? Was Linda's upbeat personality coloring her experiences, or was her job really that good? The answer, as always, is complicated.

For Linda, being treated with respect by her boss mattered. Having some say in the day-to-day operations of her work also mattered. Her experiences are supported by a great deal of research, which shows that workplace autonomy—that is, having some control over your job and some say in work processes—is related to greater worker satisfaction, better physical and mental health, and greater productivity.[4] [5] While Linda's survey responses indicated that her work scored very high on a measure of job autonomy, it was not clear at the outset what parts of the job provided that autonomy. She then told me the following story, and it started to make sense. One day, in the process of filling candle orders, Linda had begun to notice that many customers preferred certain scents or types of candles; she started giving her clients nicknames, like "hibiscus lady" and "vanilla vixen," and, on her own initiative, started adding new samples to their orders with personal notes to the customers about how they might like these new scents and products. Customers soon began to request that Linda fill their orders. Her supervisor, perplexed by these requests, called Linda into his office to ask about what was going on. When she explained her packing process, he told her that he was impressed by her creative thinking and even asked her to share with her coworkers her approach to working with "faceless" clientele. Linda was thrilled. Her boss respected her innovation, recognized her contributions, and increased her responsibility; he empowered her, while increasing sales at the same time.

There were many more examples in which Linda's boss provided emotional and financial support. For instance, Linda gave birth to a healthy baby boy, Jacob, about four weeks after our first visit. Linda told her boss that she planned to take twelve weeks off, and he let her know that he would cover her pay for any unpaid time off. She applied for and received partial disability payments, and he covered the rest, even though her company had no official paid leave policy. Once she returned to work, her boss let her leave early with no penalty if the baby was sick and gave her time during the workday to pump based on her own schedule, rather than requiring her to pump during scheduled work breaks. Linda greatly appreciated the support and, in return, was a motivated, loyal employee. As Linda's story reveals, not all low-wage work is bad work.

Contrasting the story of Linda and Mac with another young couple, Joanie and Tyler, throws into stark relief how different the experiences of low-wage work can be. Joanie shared a very different story. She worked at a privately owned grocery store, where she stocked produce. She began her shift at 4:30 a.m., lugging fruits and vegetables out from the storeroom to display. She had worked at this market since high school and, prior to getting pregnant, felt "fine" about the job. She enjoyed getting out of work in the early afternoon, and she liked her coworkers, although her boss was a real "taskmaster." When I interviewed Joanie during the third trimester of her pregnancy, she was becoming increasingly unhappy with work because her boss was unwilling to make any accommodations for her. He refused to exempt her from lifting produce boxes and did not allow her to take breaks to sit and rest. He kept a tight time schedule for prepping produce stations, and Joanie felt great pressure to finish her setups on schedule. When she asked him for a little extra prep time because her pregnancy was slowing her down a bit, he told her that if she could not keep up the pace, she should start her parental leave early, and that she could use some of her FMLA time. Using her leave while pregnant, however, would mean not only that Joanie would not be paid during this crucial period, but that she would have less time to stay home after the baby was born. She decided to stick it out and worked up to the day she gave birth. In fact, as Joanie described, she left work early that day feeling a little crampy, and their son, Skyler, was born that night at 1 a.m. She and her husband, Tyler, had saved up to be able to afford her unpaid parental leave, and she stayed home for twelve weeks. When she returned to work, things became even worse. "I went to see Jill, who handles HR paperwork. I needed to change my health insurance to add Skyler. Jill told me that Steve [their boss] had said that Skyler was not covered by my insurance. I was confused, so I went to Steve." Joanie's boss told her that she was not eligible for the family health-care plan. "He looked at me and said it was the man's job to provide health care for the family, and I should get Tyler to get health coverage. I was shocked. All the guys I worked with had health care for their kids." She sighed, "I know you think I should sue him or something, but it is not worth it. It is a job, and I need it, so I just kept my mouth shut." Joanie's job displayed the hallmarks of a bad job: low wages, low autonomy, high urgency, and an unsupportive supervisor. This is a bad formula for any worker, but especially for a new mother.

## What about the Job Matters?

These two stories highlight the highs and lows of low-income jobs. Across different low-wage occupations, the aspects of work that create autonomy, urgency, and stress vary significantly. For example, food service workers face time pressure to serve customers and often have unpredictable work hours. In contrast, certified nursing aids, who work in client's homes, tend to have stable schedules and low job stress but often feel isolated at work. Truck drivers have long, irregular work shifts, which can be quite boring, while taxi drivers work irregular hours with periods of high urgency. Thus, despite familiar stereotypes, it is inaccurate to characterize low-wage jobs as consistently mind-numbing or requiring little problem solving or engagement. Many aspects of a job come into play when considering what makes it good or bad, and we found plenty of variation within the world of low-wage work.

Measuring concepts like "job autonomy" and "time urgency" is a tricky business. What characteristics of a job, especially a low-wage job, are autonomous? What does time pressure look like in low-wage work? Most parents, however, answered these questions quite easily. As Steve said about his landscaping job, "They don't get in my way; they trust me to do my job, use my judgment, and I do it." He had job autonomy. Conversely, according to Lou, a meat cutter at a local supermarket, "They are always breathing down your neck, watching the size of your cuts, looking for waste. They don't trust no one!" Lou had little autonomy. Turning to time stress on the job, Shalonda, who worked at a fast food restaurant, described job urgency beautifully: "The clock is always running, how long did it take to get that order out, who is setting up more fries, where is my drink?" In her job, demands were fast and furious.

In our study, parents' job autonomy and urgency were assessed using two questionnaires. Job autonomy reflected the degree to which parents described their job as challenging and self-directed. They rated statements like "I have a lot of control over the way I use my time at work" and "I am able to vary the order that I complete my tasks at work each day." Parents rated their response on a five-point scale ranging from strongly disagree to strongly agree. Job urgency measured the degree to which a job required speed and time pressure. Parents rated statements like "My job requires me to work very fast most days" and "I often feel that I don't have enough time to get all my work done."

We were also interested in the types of relationships parents had on the job, so we asked a range of questions about supervisor and coworker support. Parents reported on items like "My supervisor is concerned about the welfare of those under him or her" and "My supervisor is easy to talk to." Coworkers were rated on their willingness to listen to problems and on how much they could be relied on when things got tough. Before discussing the experiences of the parents we interviewed, it is important to situate these experiences in the broader context of research examining the relationship between workers' well-being and the conditions of work.

First, much of the existing literature focuses on professional workers or compares low-wage workers to their more affluent counterparts. Few studies explore differences in experiences of control or autonomy among different types of low-income jobs, because it is often assumed there are no meaningful differences. Second, in many studies that do examine job conditions across social classes, a common approach is to measure job autonomy or urgency by assigning ratings based on job title. A professor, for example, would be assigned high autonomy scores and lower urgency scores, whereas a factory worker would be assigned low autonomy scores and high urgency scores. The problem with this approach is that it assumes that job characteristics are truly the same within occupations and that they are experienced the same way by workers within each occupation. To address these shortcomings, we looked at variability within low-income jobs, which allowed us to identify when, and under what conditions, low-wage jobs can provide autonomy and encourage positive relationships. I note this fact to emphasize that the research described below treads into relatively unexplored territory.

My main interest was to understand whether parents' reports of job autonomy, urgency, and supervisor and coworker support played any role in how well new mothers and fathers fared over the first year of parenthood. Given that our study comprised two rather distinct samples, one involving married, primarily White parents and a second with much more diversity in terms of family structure and race and ethnicity, we also had the opportunity to see if our findings replicated across these different groups. I begin by first summarizing the survey findings across samples, and then turn to parents' stories to more fully describe how work affected their lives and their children.

From our married parents, we learned, not surprisingly, that different aspects of work mattered for the men and women. For mothers, their relationships with coworkers were central. If these relationships were strong and supportive, mothers fared better in terms of their mental health. As Brianna, a manicurist, described, "These are my girls, my second family. I don't think I could do this job if they weren't here." We were surprised to find that mothers' experiences of autonomy on the job had little relation to their mental health, although there were some signals that greater autonomy was linked to lower anxiety. As the next chapter shows in detail, autonomy appears to matter more for mothers' parenting than for their mental health.

Supervisor support also mattered for mothers' mental health, especially in stressful jobs. When mothers faced mounting deadlines or stringent productivity goals, a supportive supervisor buffered the effects of the stress induced by this pressure. If mothers in high-pressure jobs had unsupportive supervisors, however, not only did they display higher levels of depression, but their depression increased over time. Moreover, many of these mothers' depressive symptoms were above the clinical cutoff for depression, meaning that they were at great risk for clinical depression. Our findings—that supervisors play a pivotal role in shaping the experiences of their workers—lend credence to a number of new experimental studies that show that training supervisors to be more supportive and attentive to employees can have positive effects on health, sleep, and well-being—and that this type of intervention may be even more important for new parents.[6]

Turning to fathers, those who reported greater autonomy—a sense of control over their work tasks and some say in daily operations—also reported more positive mental health. The more autonomy that fathers had on the job, the lower they scored on depression one year after the birth. Working in the opposite direction, the more time urgency or pressure fathers experienced at work, the higher their levels of depression. Co-worker relationships also mattered for fathers. No matter how stressful the job, if fathers felt like they had friends at work who "had their back" and "would do anything for me," their mental health was buffered from the effects of the stress. Kevin, who worked for the state Department of Public Works, talked about his "work family." "I hang out with these guys all the time. We celebrate our kids' birthdays, make a yearly trip to NASCAR races, go hunting together. They have my back, and I have theirs." This level of support at work made all the difference for Kevin when his new daughter was born. His coworkers covered his shifts for a week after the birth, so he could stay home. In contrast, fathers with low levels of coworker support who worked in highly stressful jobs reported the greatest increase in depression over the first year of parenthood.

There were also some puzzling findings. Fathers with low-urgency jobs and low coworker support reported their highest levels of depression just before birth, but their depression levels steadily declined over the first year of parenthood. Our interview with Stefan points to one possible explanation for this counterintuitive finding. Stefan worked as night security guard, a job he described as extremely boring (low urgency) and isolating. As many of the parents we interviewed described, low-urgency jobs could be "mind-numbing." When work lacks stimulation and meaning, becoming a parent fills a serious void. As Stefan told us, "Becoming a father has changed me inside and out. I do my job to support her, to make her life better. It doesn't matter if I don't love it. It matters that I am providing for her." While our study was not designed to test the significance of how parenthood shaped the experiences of parents' low-urgency work, Stefan's explanation makes sense and provides evidence for future inquiry.

What about the relationship between fathers and their supervisors? Somewhat surprisingly, supervisor support was not related to fathers' reports of their well-being. Perhaps fathers do not expect supervisors to care about their family issues and rely, instead, on support from their coworkers. Some fathers expressed distrust and suspicion of their bosses and were reluctant to share too much about themselves with their supervisors, for fear that it could be used against them in some way. A few fathers did not even tell their bosses that they were expecting a baby or had become new fathers. As CJ described, "I don't want my boss knowing my business. No reason he needs to know I am having a baby. They always want to know your business."

## Family Diversity, Mental Health, and Work-Family Relationships

Given the diversity in our second sample, in terms of both family structure and race and ethnicity, I was interested to see whether those differences mattered with respect to the impact of job experiences on parents' mental health. Would similar processes link work to family life across different family structures and families of different racial and ethnic backgrounds, or would differences be revealed?

Before reporting our results, a word of caution is needed. When comparing one social group to another (for example, Blacks and Whites, single mothers and married mothers), there is a risk of suggesting that groups are different "because of" these characteristics. Some argue that by conducting these types of analyses, researchers are complicit in reinforcing these differences and, in so doing, risk contributing to inequality. I agree that this is a risk and believe that, when researchers discuss group differences, they have an obligation to dig deeper to figure out why these differences exist. Researchers also have an obligation to look within those groups, to determine how individuals differ from one another, since averages and group differences hide individual differences that exist within groups. While it is critical to investigate whether, on average, women report higher levels of depression than men, or whether Latino fathers are more stressed than Black fathers, there is also much to be learned by examining the tremendous variability that exists within these groups. I believe the important challenge is to continually engage in both endeavors.

Regarding differences in family structure, we did not find any effects. Women who were married, cohabiting, and single displayed no meaningful differences in depression across the first year of parenthood. Interestingly, this finding flies in the face of research that suggests single mothers do less well than married or cohabiting women across a number of aspects of well-being. One possible reason for this discrepancy, as well as a reason to trust our findings over existing research, is that the mothers in our study were all low income. Comparisons between coupled and single mothers often conflate family structure with income (e.g., low-income single mothers and high-income married mothers), so the results have more to do with income than family structure. In addition, the term "single mother" implies going it alone, but many of the single mothers in our study lived with their own mothers or other kin and friends. Few were taking on the responsibilities of parenthood completely alone. Finally, the structures of many families in our study changed over time—coupled parents split up, single mothers became coupled—and we found that such *changes* in family structure, rather than the structures themselves, were related to mental health for mothers.

We did, however, uncover some interesting differences based on mothers' race and ethnicity (illustrated in figure 6). Although all mothers in our study started with high levels of depression in the months leading up to birth, African-American mothers fared the best during the first year of parenthood. As the solid line at the bottom of the graph shows, African-American mothers displayed a steep decline in depressive symptoms around the time of birth, and their symptoms stayed low throughout the following year. In contrast, Latina mothers, represented by the dotted line at the top of the graph, started their year with high levels of depression, from which they barely recovered over the course of the year. By the end of the first year, Latina mothers displayed significantly higher scores for depression than African-American mothers. As for the White mothers,

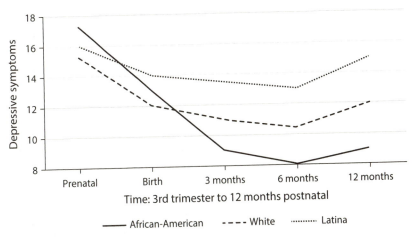

FIGURE 6. Mothers' depressive symptoms by race and ethnicity.

they began with the fewest depressive symptom, falling almost exactly between the Latina and African-American mothers by the end of the year, reporting moderate levels of depression.

How do we explain these group differences? One piece of evidence emerged when we turned to the qualitative questions we asked mothers about their work preferences. We learned that African- American mothers had rarely considered the possibility of not working. They had every expectation that they would return to work and seldomly expressed sadness or regret about doing so. As Alicia, an African-American nursing assistant, stated, "How can I be a good mother if I don't work? I have to feed her and put a roof over her head, right?" Iris, an African-American woman who worked for a pest control company, was a bit put off by the question. "All the women in my family work. My mother worked, my grandmother worked, my great grandmother worked. We work." Conversations with Latina mothers on this same topic, on the other hand, sparked tears and regrets.

As one Latina mother lamented, "How can I be a good mother if I am never there? My baby won't even know me. I would love to stay home with her, but I can't—we have to eat." The responses offered by White mothers were more varied, with some strongly preferring to work and others wishing they could stay home with their baby. Many mothers, across all races and ethnicities, reported a desire to return to paid work yet expressed the desire to stay home with their baby for a longer period before returning to work, or to return to part-time work.

One explanation for these racial and ethnic differences may reside in the unique work histories of women from these different backgrounds in the United States. On average, Latina women hold more traditional attitudes about women's roles, both in the family and in the workplace, compared to White and Black women.[7] [8] Their ambivalence about working may lead to more "negative spillover" from work to family and, consequently, result in higher levels of depression. In contrast, Black women tend to have more positive attitudes about balancing work and family and being economic providers than White women (no research to date has compared the views of Black and Latina women).[9] [10] These data highlight not only intriguing differences but also the lack of research regarding the ways in which cultural differences shape the connections between work and family.[11]

## Work and Family Relations among Diverse Families

We had the opportunity with our second, more diverse sample to explore more deeply the connections between work and family life among single parents and cohabiting parents, as well as among Latino, White, and Black parents. In many ways, the story looked the same. No matter the mothers' race or family structure, job conditions such as autonomy or work relationships mattered for mothers' well-being. But families in our second sample did differ in some important ways. More mothers in this sample worked part-time, and they moved into and out of jobs much more frequently. In addition, parents' relationships were less stable, and many moved into and out of different living situations numerous times over the first year. Their stories make clear that these differences are intimately linked to economic security and work conditions.

In an effort to see if we could replicate some of the results described from our married sample, we first looked at mothers' experiences of job pressure and urgency. We found that holding down a high-pressure job was related not only to higher overall levels of depression, but also to increases in depression across the first year of parenthood. Surprisingly, these effects were the most pronounced for mothers who worked part-time. Why is this? One might think (as I did) that part-time work would be protective in this situation, since it would afford greater flexibility and time at home. Angela, a single mother who worked as a telemarketer, offers one possible explanation. In her office, a big screen highlighted how many sales you made during your shift, so the pressure and job urgency were intense. Although she had been promised full-time hours when she took the job, Angela rarely received more than thirty hours per week and often far fewer. Thus, she was working too few hours, which created financial strain, and she was doing a highly stressful job, which negatively affected her well-being. We learned that many mothers who worked part-time desperately wanted and needed more hours of work. Renee liked working as a cashier at a big box store, and her supervisor continually held out the promise of more hours, but she had not seen them yet. "I can't survive on twenty to twenty-five hours

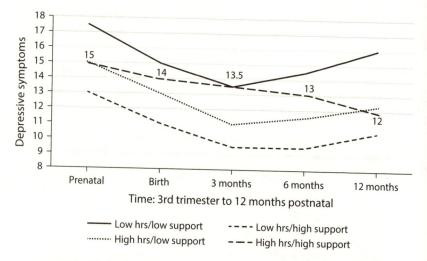

FIGURE 7. Mothers' supervisor support, work hours, and depressive symptoms.

a week. I am a good worker, and I want to work, but they just won't give me full-time."

We learned, however, that these negative aspects of works could be counterbalanced by supportive supervisors. As is shown in figure 7, mothers with both low work hours and low supervisor support (solid black line) reported the highest levels of depressive symptoms across the first year of parenthood. In contrast, mothers with low hours and high supervisor support had the lowest symptoms (bottom short-dashed line).

Lindi worked part-time at a laundromat after her baby's birth, and at work she washed and folded clothes. Her boss let her set her own schedule, and, if she needed, she could bring the baby to work. "He is really so great," said Lindi. "He knows this won't be forever, and he just wants me to get the job done." Mothers with full-time jobs and supportive supervisors experienced a decline in depressive symptoms throughout the year, but they were not doing as well as mothers who worked part-time with good supervisors.

One important aspect of work life that is not captured by these data is the extent to which work hours ebb and flow based on employers' needs and desires. Rachel, who worked as a server for events at a hotel, described the stress caused by unpredictable hours and a supervisor who did not seem to care. "You just can't plan, you can't plan. So over Christmas and New Year's, I was working sixty hours a week; the job was intense. We did not have enough workers, and the pressure was crazy. I was so stressed, and my supervisor would not give me a break. Now that the holidays are over, I am lucky if I get twenty hours a week. The days are slow, and I often get sent home early. That is how it goes. You never know how much money you will have week to week. It is so stressful." A lack of stability in hours made it extremely difficult for parents to plan their lives. Imagine trying to make child-care plans when you don't know if you will be working twenty hours or fifty hours the next week, or trying to plan a budget when you have no idea how much money you will bring home any given week. Unsurprisingly, this instability was harmful to workers—the more unstable parents' work hours, the less autonomy and less support they reported.

In sum, work hours, urgency, and supports can vary significantly over time. Snapshots gleaned from survey data often cannot capture the dynamic nature of these jobs, especially those in jobs where demands and hours shift seasonally, or even weekly. Few professional workers would stand for this type of uncertainty, yet it is often the nature of the job for many low-wage workers.

## Parents' Experiences of Low-Wage Jobs: Autonomy, Urgency, and Support

In the previous section, I reviewed findings from the standardized surveys used to assess parents reports of autonomy, urgency, and support. Although informative, I found this approach failed to capture the richness of the experiences parents shared with me about their jobs, what made them autonomous or stressful. In the next section, I use parents' stories to bring to life what autonomy, urgency, and support on the job look like for factory workers, certified nursing assistants (CNAs), food service workers, and others.

Turning first to autonomy, it is most often defined by academics as having control over how you do your job, variety in what you do at work, and the sense that your work contributes to a common goal. Conversely, low-autonomy jobs are characterized by performing the same activity, again and again, with little chance for problem solving, input, or stimulation. Compared to professional jobs, low-wage jobs are, on average, lower in autonomy. But as discussed earlier, averages can mask dramatic differences in individual experiences; such was the case with the parents we interviewed, who described a wide range of conditions at work.

Among our participants, fast food service workers, cashiers, and bank tellers reported the lowest levels of autonomy on the job. As noted earlier, jobs in the fast food industry were often the most challenging. Kiely, who worked at KFC, described her job in the following way: "I could really be a robot, take order, fill order, hand order over, smile, and act like you care." Combine this lack of autonomy with the urgency often required by fast food work, and you have the ingredients for a stressful and potentially harmful job. In these contexts, the role of one's boss can make all the difference. Kiely, however, described her boss as "checked out" and spending much of his time smoking behind the restaurant.

We also talked to parents who reported a significant amount of autonomy at work. When we met Hank, he was a salesperson at a large sports store, but he was being trained for a supervisory role. He felt that his job held great promise, and he was excited about being given a new level of responsibility. As he explained, "I'm in training for an area manager position. Right now, it's a comanager position, which is right under a store manager level. But I'm being trained in many different stores, being exposed to different types of management and underneath the district manager. She has been phenomenal, very understanding, very caring and, four months ago, was very eager to recruit me into the company, so she kind of wants to make sure she keeps ahold of me." Hank felt valued at work. On top of that, he was in a stimulating environment, learning new things. Even though Hank was unhappy that he was only making $9.50 an hour, he liked his job and thought he had a future in front of him.

Job urgency, which I described above as the sense of pressure and time constraints under which one works, comes in several distinct forms: being overscheduled, having too much to do in too short of a period, having high rates for the amount of work that needs to be completed in a day, or being the only worker with your skill set. The interesting thing about urgency is that one wants neither too much nor too little of it in a job. Jobs where one feels no pressure to complete tasks can quickly become boring, while jobs with unreasonable time goals can be too stressful. As with job autonomy, urgency varies significantly among low-income jobs.

Phil worked as a mechanic, a job he loved, but which came with a good deal of pressure. "Due to the amount of work and my position as a mechanic, and as one of the better ones that takes on the bigger jobs, it was hard to get time off for the birth. Because you know, like I said, there's nobody just to say we will come in and fill in for this guy while he's out, because you know, he's got a family reason. They did give me some hassle. They gave me the time; they didn't have a choice; I just didn't go into work. I told them I'd come in when I'm ready." Since Phil was recognized as a valuable worker in his shop, he was able to demand the time he needed after the birth. This was not the case for most workers, including Sarah, who worked as a field representative assistant for a drug company. Her job required her to travel quite a bit in order to set up displays and sell products with her managers. Although she was not directly responsible for selling products, the team she worked with faced constant pressure to sell and hit quotas, which was conveyed to her every day. The pressure at her job was high, and the level of support was extremely low. "It's totally like push the mothers out. Because you can't dedicate as much time, they can't get as much from you when you have a kid. You can't hit your mark as quickly. Whereas if you're a single employee they can suck you dry time-wise."

The idea that hourly jobs are performed only at work—that when a worker leaves for the day, the job is left behind—was a notion refuted by the experiences of many parents in the study. Andy worked as an information clerk at an insurance agency, which involved reviewing claims, organizing files, and typing summaries. He described needing to bring work home to get it all done, cutting into the little time he had with his new son. "Well, my work has been very, very busy lately, which has put a lot of pressure on me. I mean, I take a lot of work home 'cause I have work that's—we build it up as we go to work each day. It's got to be completed by turnaround time, and we're in very busy part of the season right now. Things are building up. I get out of work at like eight o'clock, and I come home, and I want to spend time with Nicholas, you know, but I don't see him for ten and a half hours, 'cause I leave really early in the morning." Like Andy, many who worked at insurance companies or other offices would bring home paperwork to finish for the next day.

Others, like certified nursing assistants, would take calls from their clients at home. These workers were not paid for hours worked at home, but they felt working at home was necessary in order to stay caught up on work. Parents who worked as cooks, servers, mechanics, and factory workers, on the other hand, described their jobs as tied to the workplace; when they went home, the job was over.

As discussed earlier, in the face of low autonomy and high job urgency, the role of supervisors and coworkers can make a tremendous difference. Supportive relationships can protect against stressful jobs, while unsupportive relationships can exacerbate the misery imposed by these conditions. We found that for mothers, but not fathers, relationships with supervisors mattered the most. Mothers described a vast array of experiences ranging from supervisors who expressed concern and bent the rules to accommodate new parents, to those who were impatient, critical, and rigid. Some supervisors were revered, while others were held in great disdain. Cayla, a file clerk at the local hospital, had only good things to say about her manager. "My manager just puts families first. Families come before anything else. If you have a family issue or anything, she'll do her best to work with you. . . . I think a lot of what makes my job good is my manager. It just makes our workplace more effective. Like if we have a hostile environment, we're not going to want to go in, so, she makes it a friendly environment, you know, where we can go to her for anything. It just makes it a lot easier. I love it. Like I have never loved a job so much in my life." Shannon, an office assistant who primarily answered phones, scheduled meetings, and served as a receptionist, also gave her supervisor high marks. "He's really good if I need to leave early or . . . especially with me cutting back to thirty-five hours instead of forty. He just signed the paper and didn't make it hard for me at all.

And he really works with me to try to make sure that I'm not too stressed. He even asks me [laughs] like once a week he asks how I'm doing." It was not uncommon for new parents to share stories about supervisors who asked them about their family life, checked in about their baby, and made efforts to ease their transition back to work. We heard stories about supervisors who sent meals to their employees after their baby was born, who continued to pay employees even though it was not policy, and who let parents bring the baby to work during the early months after birth.

Although these stories of support are heartening, we also heard an equal share of stories describing the ways in which supervisors had little concern for their workers as parents. John felt that his boss "couldn't care less" about him or his family. He described how scary the birth had been. His wife, Mary, went into labor three weeks early, and their baby, Riley, was born with some respiratory issues. There was meconium in the amniotic fluid, a condition that can partly, or completely, block the baby's airway, and Riley spent three nights in the ICU after the birth. As John described it, "We didn't get out of the hospital until Tuesday or Wednesday of the following week after the baby was born. We both got off so we could stay with her [the baby] while she was in ICU. But that whole time my foreman was on the phone trying to get me to come back to work. My baby was in the ICU. . . . They really don't care."

Gerry worked as a security guard at a casino and talked about how, depending on the time of year, supervisors were more or less lenient. As he explained, the casino was always busy around the holidays. During Thanksgiving, Christmas, and New Year's there was no leniency with respect to his work schedule, but things were better after the new year. When I asked him whether he thought his company was responsive to his family responsibilities, he described how their actions didn't always match their words. "There was an incident where Kristin's grandmother passed away, and they gave me one day for a death in the family, and Kristin's grandmother was actually closer to me than my own grandmother was. So, the day that I took off was actually the day that she died. The next day I was trying to get everything together with the wake and all that. I really needed those extra couple days, and they were completely against giving me those days. They were going to discipline me if I took those days because they said that I was only allowed one day, and that's because it was really busy at work."

When we asked parents if policies that supervisors were instituting were official policies or informal decisions made on the fly, many parents did not know the answer. For example, one supervisor falsely told Jennifer, who had worked at the same department store for the past two years, that she was ineligible to use FMLA policies because she had not been with the company for five years. Jennifer felt uncomfortable challenging her boss on this issue, so she exhausted her vacation and sick time and returned to work three weeks after giving birth. In some cases, supervisors offered policies to some employees but not others, with little explanation or justification. Phil, the mechanic introduced earlier, described what he saw as preferential treatment. Given his value to the company, he was able to take time off after the birth of his child, while the secretary in the front office lost a day's pay when she stayed home with her sick baby.

## Autonomy and Support without High Pay

Does it make sense to talk about positive job conditions when a primary condition of employment—making a livable wage—is not met? Does it matter if you have things like a supportive supervisor or autonomy on your job if you make minimum wage? The data and stories I have shared may appear to suggest that good work is not primarily about the money, but about people's experiences at work. In fact, it is about *both* of these things. According to the latest data from the Bureau of Labor Statistics, five of the fastest growing occupations in the country have annual salaries below $25,000.[12] These include food prep and service workers, personal care aides, home health aides, retail sales people, and restaurant cooks—also the most common occupations among the parents we interviewed for this project. Low-wage work does not appear to be disappearing anytime soon, so where should policy efforts focus moving forward? I would argue that change must be pursued on every front. On the income and wages front, the living wage movement, which began in the early 1990s, is a growing grassroots effort aimed at creating a true livable wage that "allows workers and families to be self sufficient at a basic needs level (food, housing, clothing, transportation—with no frills)."[13] Across the country, living wage coalitions, composed of community organizations, unions, faith-based organizations, and progressive legal groups, have organized to introduce and pass living wage ordinances. Although the federal minimum wage still sits at $7.25 an hour, cities, state, and individual companies have imposed higher wage floors. As countless CEOs and politicians have argued, a living wage is good for business because it results in less turnover, greater consumer spending, and increases in home ownership. Wages mattered for all the parents I talked to: having a baby is an expensive proposition. More than 80 percent of those we interviewed were stressed about making ends meet.

Along with increasing wages, however, our research demonstrates the importance of improving workers' experiences on the job. What can be done to increase a worker's sense of control and autonomy, to hold job urgency in check, and to create supportive work environments? New research points to some interesting ways to bring about change at this level. Research involving a large IT firm has shown that better training and support for midlevel supervisors—training focused on communication, work flow, and support—resulted in better outcomes for workers.[14] Successful interventions with supervisors have also improved work satisfaction among physicians.[15]

Less research has been conducted involving low-income workers. However, interventions focused on reducing work-family strain among workers in retail stores and grocery stores have yielded positive results in terms of employee retention and work-family balance.[16] [17] During my own earlier research with a food plant in the Midwest, I was asked to help resolve a challenging work scheduling issue that resulted from mandatory overtime. Workers were consistently being told, with no warning, that they needed to stay late to finish an order. This policy, although legal, was creating significant unrest among the workers, many of whom had young children who needed to be picked up from day care or school. In an attempt to understand the problem better, I held a focus group with workers and asked them if they had thoughts about how to solve the problem. Of course they did. They proposed that each worker have set "on-call" days for overtime, which allowed workers to plan ahead; it was that simple. The company agreed to institute a trial period to test out the policy. The proposed plan worked beautifully, and it was soon adopted as company policy. This collaborative process not only solved a pressing workplace problem but empowered workers. The lesson is clear: give workers a voice in problem solving, and the solutions might just stick.

An important takeaway message from the data and stories shared in this chapter is that what happens at work matters.

Wages matter; time away from work—in the form of parental leave, personal time, and sick time—also clearly matters, and I and others have written much about solutions for giving parents time away from the job to be parents. But, we must also pay attention to what happens on the job that affects parents and their parenting. Addressing issues of job autonomy, urgency, and support at work not only is good for employees but provides some solutions for employers. Employees who feel supported and are respected as key players in the organization are more satisfied, loyal, and willing to stay in the job, no matter what the job. My recommendations for how to use these findings to inform workplace polices are laid out in detail in chapter 7, but, focusing on parents' day-in-and-day-out experiences on the job may be as important as our efforts to give parents time away from work.

## Linda and Mac: One Year as Workers and Parents

In my final interview with Linda, the woman who loved her job in the candle-packing factory, her one-year-old, Jacob, was just beginning to walk and charmed us with his ability to pull apart our interview folders in record time. I sat down to talk with Linda to see how the year had gone. As always, she was upbeat. "We are doing well. Jacob is a joy, and we have been thinking about when baby number two might happen." Things at work were also continuing to go well: "It is great. Business is booming, and they are constructing a new building that will have better light and temperature control . . . and, I got a raise. There is a lot of pressure, but we are making it happen." Her responses were a bit more sober when we discussed the demands of parenting. "Jacob is getting a little more challenging and, sometimes, after a long day, it is hard to have the energy to be his mom. I know we let him watch too much TV. Mac and I talk about that a lot." She sounded tired. "Anyone can be a parent, but to be a good parent you really have to get in there, be engaged, roll around on the floor, read books . . . all that stuff. Sometimes I have to push Mac to turn off the TV and just play with Jacob."

From Mac's perspective, things were going well. He felt like he and Linda were a great team and successfully balancing their jobs, their relationship, and their responsibilities as parents. But he also acknowledged the challenges. "Linda is kind of a 'glass-half-full person.' She works hard to make it all look easy . . . and it is not really easy at all. It is worth it, for sure, but it is not easy." Although Mac had been reluctant to participate when we first met, he had turned into quite the talker over the course of the year and shared his concerns about his job. He continued to work for the town maintenance department and was very worried about budget cutbacks and layoffs. He wasn't concerned for himself, since he had seven years of seniority, but was worried about some of his coworkers, who might lose their job in the next round of cuts. "Sometimes the stress gets to me. I don't want to see my buddies lose their jobs." Parenting was also a challenge. "As I said in the beginning, it is worth it, but it is hard. Being a good parent is hard, even under the best of circumstances. I could probably do better. I need to play more, turn off the TV. . . . I am sure Linda brought that up. I think it will get easier as he gets older, and I can take him fishing and hunting and do things together."

Work spills over into family life in numerous ways: by sapping one's energy, influencing one's mood, and limiting one's time. As both Mac and Linda described, new parents' high aspirations for parenting can be hard to live up to at times. When work is stressful or demoralizing, parents often struggle to muster the energy to engage with an energetic, curious, and emotional baby. This happens to all parents from time to time. Concern arises when it happens too often. When tired or over-whelmed parents start to consistently "check out" or become short-tempered, the family suffers. In the next chapter, we dig into the topic of parenting and examine how work affects the quality and quantity of parenting that children receive.

# CHAPTER 5

# "This Parenting Thing Is Harder Than It Looks"

*Low-Income Work and Parenting*

Ellen lived in a gritty, working-class suburb outside of the city. Our first interview took place in her tiny, sparsely furnished studio apartment, which she had moved into only a month earlier. The living-room area contained an oversized couch, a large TV, and a crate that served as a coffee table, while her little kitchen area had a rickety card table and two mismatched chairs. I found out later that the couch also served as Ellen's bed. I asked Ellen if Roy, her boyfriend, was going to join us at any point. When we had scheduled the interview, she told me that he might be willing to talk with me. As it turned out, he would not be coming. They had been fighting, and Ellen told me, reluctantly, that she was going to be a young, single mother at the age of twenty-two. When Ellen had informed Roy that she was pregnant, he had not been happy. She hoped he "would come around eventually," but at the present moment, he had no interest in being a dad, and no interest in talking with me.

"So, tell me about your job?" I asked. Ellen told me that she worked the night shift as a certified nursing assistant at a nearby nursing home. She walked to work, since she did not own a car, which was the main reason for her recent move. She made $10 an hour and was three months into a six-month waiting period before she was eligible for health-care and vacation benefits. She described her job as lonely and boring; her main tasks involved paperwork, helping residents to the bathroom, personal care for clients, cleaning, and redirecting wandering residents. Ellen had saved up enough money to take four weeks of unpaid leave when the baby was born, after which she planned to return to work. Her mother, who lived in Boston, planned to be with Ellen during the birth and to stay with her for her first week as a new mother. Her child-care plan was still up in the air, since finding nighttime infant care presents unique challenges. Ellen was hopeful that plans with a friend, who had said she might be willing to take care of the baby at night, would work out. The details, however, were far from settled.

Even before looking at Ellen's responses to the mental health questionnaires, I knew she was depressed. She talked in a soft monotone, her expressions were flat, and she was heartbroken over her recent breakup with Roy. She had fantasies that after the baby was born her boyfriend might have a change of heart and return to her. "Maybe he is just scared. Maybe when he sees the baby, he will love it and want to do the right thing." She had few friends, and most of her family, including her mother, brother, and aunt, lived two hours away. She had no contact with her father. Ellen had a hard time expressing any emotion about the upcoming birth, either fear or excitement. For the most part, her answers were short and to the point. While she didn't want to talk about what was coming, there was a clear sense of impending doom about how her life was going to play out in the upcoming months.

In the following chapter, I explore how work affects parenting. Will Ellen's job—both the hours and the schedule, but also the boredom and the dissatisfaction—have any effect on her ability to be a caring and engaged new mother? Research consistently shows that parents' employment—the simple fact of holding down a paid job—has few *direct* effects on children's development. For example, parents' work hours, looked at in isolation, explain very little about the variation in children's development. But, and this is a big "but," this does not mean that parents' work does not matter for children. What it means is that, with respect to children's development, the raw number of hours worked matters less than what happens during those hours. In chapters 3 and 4, I presented evidence showing how work policies and conditions affect mothers' and fathers' mental health. In this chapter, we examine how these policies and conditions influence the quality of their parenting. Poor work conditions can chip away at a worker's vitality, morale, and overall well-being and, by doing so, deplete their energy for parenting. Ellen's story is one of the most extreme examples I witnessed of this phenomenon.

When I returned for my next visit with Ellen, after her baby's birth, things looked vastly different. The birth had changed Ellen. Sitting on the couch, cuddling her beautiful baby girl, Eva, Ellen seemed content. Her mother, who had come to visit for the weekend, was doing dishes at the kitchen sink and came over to introduce herself. She was glad I had arrived since it gave her a chance to run out to do a few errands while Ellen and I talked. Ellen was still a bit subdued, but it seemed as if a cloud had lifted. She smiled a bit, bragged about what a good eater Eva was, and was quite proud to tell me she had pushed only four times during labor before her baby "popped out." Roy, Eva's father, had started coming around every few days to see her, and

Ellen was hopeful that they would get back together. Ellen had decided to take off three more weeks than originally planned and would head back to work when Eva was seven weeks old. As Ellen had hoped, her friend, who lived in the same apartment complex, was willing to take care of the baby at night while Ellen was at work. After listening to Ellen's plan, I asked her when she was planning to sleep. "Well, my plan right now is to sleep when she sleeps. I will come home and feed her and sleep while she naps. Then I can take a nap in the afternoon when she sleeps. I don't need much sleep. It will be fine." The plan seemed destined for failure. The idea that she could care for herself and a new baby and hold down a full-time job while sleeping about four hours each day seemed unrealistic. I said my good-byes and let Ellen know that I would be calling soon to see how the transition to work was going.

Six weeks later, on a freezing November morning, I drove down to meet with Ellen again. She had been back at work for four weeks. I knocked on the door of her apartment and heard a muffled "come in." I cracked open the door to a dark room, the only light coming from a small nightlight shining in the corner. Ellen was lying on the couch with the baby wrapped in her arms. "Hi," I said, "are you still up for this interview?" Ellen whispered, "Sure, just nodded off while I was waiting." I walked in and closed the door. In the shadows, I saw a mound of dirty clothes spilling out of a laundry basket next to the couch, and the apartment smelled like dirty diapers and cigarettes. Ellen had arrived home from her night shift at 7 a.m. that morning, and Eva had only taken catnaps all morning. She expected the baby would sleep through our interview. I told Ellen that we could easily reschedule if she wanted to sleep. "No, I like the company."

As we started to talk, Ellen described how overwhelming things had become since returning to work. Her child-care situation seemed to be working. Eva slept at her friend's apartment five nights each week. The baby took one bottle during the night, and her friend reported that, besides the one feeding, she was sleeping through the night fairly regularly. The problem for Ellen was that the baby was taking two naps during the day, each of which lasted only about an hour and half. This meant that Ellen was functioning on about three to four hours of sleep. It showed. Slouched on the couch, with dark circles under her eyes, she looked exhausted. I asked her how she was doing. "Not so good, I guess. This is hard. It is so hard. Roy has disappeared. All I do is go to work, come home, take care of her, try to sleep and go back to work. Work is short-handed, and they want me to work more hours, and I can't. They are not too happy with me." We sat there quiet for a moment, and Ellen mumbled, "There is just nothing to look forward to."

This third interview with parents included an eight-minute parent-child interaction task, which we would record. When baby Eva woke up halfway through the interview, I asked Ellen if she would be willing to do the activity with Eva. She agreed. I placed Eva in a baby seat in front of her mother, and I asked Ellen to interact and engage with Eva in her typical way, whatever that was. I set up the camera and busied myself with paperwork on the couch. Our normal procedure involved having the interviewer leave the room to give the parents some privacy, but since Ellen lived in a studio apartment, that was not possible. As I peeked at the mother and baby playing, I noticed Ellen staring off into space as Eva tried to catch her attention. Then Ellen pulled out her phone and started checking messages. She leaned over and kissed Eva, but then ignored Eva's attempt to reach out to her mother with her tiny hands. Ellen was distracted and disengaged. As Eva wiggled around in her seat and made little grunting sounds to attract her mother's attention,

Ellen put her hand on her leg but continued to check her phone. It was a long, sad eight minutes to witness.

Ellen's story is devastating because it marks the beginning of a parent-child interaction pattern that, if not interrupted, is likely to have profound implications for Eva's development. Child psychologists use terms like "maternal sensitivity" or "maternal attunement" to capture parent-child interactions where mothers are sensitive to their child's moods and interests. When parents are attuned, they use eye contact, touch, and voice tone to engage the child and support his or her behaviors. Ellen was not attuned to Eva as I watched her that day; she was simply too tired and depressed to engage with Eva, even while being filmed. This is one way that a parent's job can affect a child: it can hinder a parent's ability to be warm, caring, and engaged. This has nothing to do with how much Ellen loved her child, as there was no doubt that Ellen completely and fully loved her daughter. Ellen was recovering physically from childbirth, functioning day in and day out on about four hours of sleep, raising a child with only a weak support network, and working at a demanding and unsupportive job. This situation was taking a serious toll on her well-being, as well as the quality of her parenting.

As we witnessed with many of our families, long work hours in stressful jobs can leave parents feeling tired and depleted when they arrive home, which makes it difficult to summon the energy needed to care for an infant. Similarly, shift work that requires evening and night hours can lead to exhaustion and lethargy on the home front. Beyond hours and schedules, our research finds that low levels of autonomy, unsupportive supervisors, and poor coworker relations similarly interfere with a new parent's ability to come home ready to feed, change, bathe, cuddle, and play with their baby. One way that parents' work is transmitted to their children, according to our data, is through its impact on parents' mental health. Another way that parents' work is transmitted to their children is through its impact on their parenting abilities and styles. It is important to note that although parents' good mental health is often related to sensitive parenting, mental health and parenting can also act independently. For instance, interventions aimed at reducing maternal depression immediately before and after birth are effective in reducing depressive symptoms, but they do not, necessarily, improve parenting skills. More generally, depressed parents can sometimes be sensitive parents,[1] while nondepressed parents can be insensitive caregivers. While it is true that maternal and paternal depression can interfere with sensitive parenting, this is not the only path that connects work conditions and parenting quality. Work conditions can also directly affect parenting behavior, quite apart from its impact on parents' mental health. As Ellen's story illustrates, poor working conditions can lead to things going terribly wrong; but work can also have positive effects on parenting, effects that bode well for children's social and emotional development.

## The Meaning of Parenthood for Working Mothers and Fathers

In order to understand the relationship between parents' jobs and their parenting, it is important to understand, first, what being a parent means to new mothers and fathers, and how they conceive the obligations of that role. When we asked participants in our study what it meant to be a parent, some (more often women) would say that being a parent means to be "caring," "loving," "all in," and "sacrificing." For others (more often men), being a good parent meant being a "good provider," "putting a roof over their heads," and "being responsible." Thus, for this latter group, going to work and being financially responsible defined a core feature of good parenting, while for the former group, these behaviors are unrelated to parenting. Not surprisingly, there were clear gender differences in how men and women talked about parenting.

We asked mothers and fathers several questions about their expectations regarding their new roles: What are the responsibilities of being a mother/father? What behaviors do you do to be a good mom or dad? And do moms and dads do different things? The majority of parents, both mothers and fathers, had little trouble describing the role of a mother. Jill, who worked as a "cleaning agent" for a large cleaning company, responded, "Being a parent, to me, is caring for your child's needs; being there when your child needs you, when she cries be there for her; not put others first. My main and first priority is my daughter. So, I guess that, to me, is what being a parent means. Nothing comes first but her." According to Sheila, a mother's job was "to take care of children, to be responsible for them mentally, emotionally. To put them above you. To just make sure they are given the best opportunities and teach them the best that I can." For Carmen, being a mother "means a lot. It means giving up yourself for other people. You let them have all your time." Almost everyone agreed that mothers were selfless, all-giving, all-knowing, almost saint-like; and, if they weren't, they were striving to be.

When asked about the specific responsibilities tied to the role of mother, most mentioned everyday child-care responsibilities like feeding, diapering, bathing, and taking children to doctor appointments. When Diana was asked about her responsibilities, she hesitated a bit, then said, "Being with the kids, feeding the kids, taking care of them, doctor's appointments, dentist appointments, pretty much everything [laughs]." Another mother stated, "You know, the one to cook, clean, take care of the house, take care of someone when they're sick; they never take their father too serious."

Fathers often alluded to the unique bond between mothers and their infants. As Jamar stated, "Mothers have a whole, a bit of a different angle on parenting. I think mothers might feel a little closer to their child; they did the caring for nine months, so I can see that happening. Mothers are an important thing—that's all I have to say." Fathers talked about mothers as "the glue," "the heart," and "the moral compass" of the home. As Guy stated, "She keeps us together . . . mellow, calm. . . . She thinks a little bit more about what's ahead. She's rational about things. She's even-tempered. She keeps the atmosphere level. No combustion."

There was less agreement about fathers' roles and responsibilities. When Guy was asked about his role as a father, he said, quite simply, "Financial provider. Keep the bills organized . . . our life organized." Similarly, Sully stated that while mothers need to "keep them safe and full and warm and clean," his job was to "make sure you got a safe home to live in, you got plenty of food, but keeping them safe is the main thing." According to Gina, "Darryl's most important role . . . in my family . . . I look at him more as being a helper for me, rather than just a parent. Like I feel sometimes that I'm her mom and her dad. Even though he's here, and he's helping and everything, just sometimes I feel like I want, I want to be more for her than anybody else. But I look at him to help me more when it comes to my needs. Yeah, the baby needs him, and he's there for her, but I also need him." Brittany quickly responded, "Discipline and also the parenting—with a father's perspective." What does it mean to parent with a "father's perspective"? According to Brittany, fathers need to be the strict parent, the one who laid down the law and stuck with it. Despite the fact that nearly all mothers and fathers in our study went back to work soon after their child's birth, and most families could not have survived without two incomes, many held gendered expectations about fathers being economic providers and mothers being caretakers. For example, Sharonne worked full-time at the airport as a cabin cleaner on a plane and brought home 60 percent of the family income, but when asked about her boyfriend's responsibilities as a dad, she succinctly responded, "To provide for the family and . . . that's it." When the interviewer asked about her role as a provider, she said, "I just do the job to make ends meet."

There were some parents, a clear minority, who countered these traditional narratives with strong views about the importance of equality in parenting. For example, Paul stated, "It doesn't matter if you're male/female—both share the same responsibilities. Being a parent is to share the duties that come along with being a parent. From diaper changing to getting up at night to making formula, soothing the baby, it's just cut right down the middle, you know, not one of us does something more than the other. And I think that's important. And then working, ah, both need to be getting an income. So, you know, you have to both do it. So we really look at it that way. We both have to do it. Go to work and both provide. No one's slacking."

The parental expectations that you have for yourself and your partner will influence the ways in which work shapes your involvement in parenting. For example, if, like many of the mothers we talked to, you expect to "be everything to everyone," the bar is set quite high for parenthood. If, on the other hand, you believe in an equal division of labor, the experience of being a new parent may be quite different. Fathers and mothers who hold more egalitarian views about parenthood share child care more equally, and fathers who have less gendered ideas about "who should do what" end up performing more child care during the first year of their child's life.[2]

Looking beyond gender differences, Annette Lareau highlights social class differences in beliefs about parenting in her well-known book *Unequal Childhoods* (2003). In her field research with Black and White school-aged children from middle-class, working-class, and poor families, she describes distinctly different beliefs and behaviors about parenting. The middle-class parents she interviewed practiced what she labeled "concerted cultivation," where parents organized children's lives around after-school programming and enrichment activities and provided structure to help their children excel. The working class and poor, by contrast, relied on the "accomplishment of natural growth," where children had more freedom, less parental monitoring, and fewer opportunities for structured activities than their more affluent counterparts. Lareau argues that, in terms of parenting, it appears that differences in class overshadowed differences in race.[3] While Lareau's research describes class differences among parents with school-aged children, what might these differences look like for families caring for infants? Are there class differences that affect parenting styles during this crucial period of development? Since our study focused exclusively on working-class families, we could not compare across class levels as Lareau did, but we did gain some insights into how working-class parents think about and enact parenting with their infants. The parents we talked with all wanted to be good parents and provide the best for their children, but there was tremendous variability in what that parenting looked like across families, as discussed further below.

## What We Know about Work and Parenting

The question of how work affects parenting and child development has received tremendous attention over the years. As women entered the workforce in great numbers in the 1960s and 1970s, there was widespread concern that their children might be harmed by the lack of maternal care. Hundreds of studies explored how parents' employment, or to be more accurate, how mothers' employment, was related to maternal-child attachment, maternal sensitivity, child behavior problems, school achievement, peer relationships, and even college graduation rates. Although some studies did find small positive or negative effects of maternal work hours on some child outcomes, the most consistent finding was that maternal work hours, in and of themselves, were unrelated to children's developmental outcomes. As I indicated earlier, this conclusion should not be interpreted as implying that maternal employment does not matter for children. It simply means that work hours alone are not an important factor. To understand how employment affects parenting, one must instead look more closely at the different conditions of employment as they shape mothering and fathering.[4][5]

During the 1980s and 1990s, research on maternal employment became more nuanced, and researchers began to examine characteristics of the jobs performed by mothers, in addition to hours worked. Studies documented that the nature of work—for example, the extent to which it was stimulating and complex—was more important to the quality of mothers' parenting than raw work hours.[6][7][8] Two work-family sociologists, Toby Parcel and Elizabeth Menaghan (1994), wrote an influential book, *Parents' Jobs and Children's Lives*, that documented that work that requires independent thinking and problem solving, what they called occupational complexity, was linked to more positive home environments—homes, for example, that had more books and cognitively stimulating toys. Studies also showed that mothers and fathers with more complex and stimulating jobs used less restrictive parenting styles with their school-aged children.[9] [10] [11] This early research revealed that when mothers experience more autonomy at work, they tend to engage in more proactive and supportive parenting behaviors at home.

Less research has explored how parents' work conditions shape parenting during the sensitive first year of a child's life, although this topic has recently started to receive more attention. Some research shows that, for mothers but not fathers, positive relationships at work yield more positive forms of parenting during this formative period.[12] Additionally, little work has delved into social class differences in how work is related to early parenting. However, research by Ben Goodman and colleagues has shown that low-income fathers who demonstrated self-direction at work engaged in higher-quality parenting with their infants.[13] [14] Another study, in which mothers recorded their experiences in low-wage jobs (i.e., negative interactions with a supervisor) and their interactions at home with their child in a daily diary, found that the more criticism mothers experienced from supervisors on a given day, the more withdrawn and harsh the mothers were at home.[15] Although these studies differ from one another in a variety of ways, all provide some evidence for a relationship between work and parenting quality.

## What Is Parenting Quality?

Family researchers have been measuring "parenting quality" for decades. Although there is no consensus on the best measure(s) of good parenting, there is broad agreement on some of its central ingredients, including warmth and responsiveness. Warmth refers to sensitive, loving, caring behaviors expressed by caregivers to their young. This includes warmth demonstrated through touch (hugs, stroking, cuddling), voice (high pitched, engaging), and visual contact (eye contact, expressive interactions). Although many studies rely on parents' own reports of how warm and sensitive they are with their children, most researchers agree that observing parents interact with their children in natural settings is the best way to assess parenting—the "gold standard" in parenting research. During our home visits with families, we asked parents to play with a new toy with their baby, a giraffe rattle, and instructed them to simply interact with their baby as they normally would. We recorded these play sessions and, afterward, coded them for different aspects of parenting behavior. For example, we assessed the tone of their voices, how often they touched their child, the type of language they used, and how much they engaged. We coded four primary types of behavior: responsiveness, detachment, intrusiveness, and stimulation. Each is described below.

*Responsiveness* refers to how sensitive, prompt, and responsive parents are with their infants. Highly responsive parents are quick to provide encouragement or support when their infant is frustrated. In contrast, *detachment* measures parents' physical and emotional engagement (or lack thereof) with their baby, including eye contact, verbal interaction, and warmth. For example, Ellen, the mother I described earlier in this chapter, often ignored Eva's "bids" for her mother's attention (low responsiveness); however, she also exhibited some behaviors that looked responsive, like touching and hugging (high responsiveness). However, Ellen's behavioral responsiveness often came with a lack of warmth and connection (high detachment). She was highly detached and low on responsiveness in her interactions—busy looking at her phone, distracted by TV, and ignoring her child's attempts to get her attention. *Intrusiveness* refers to controlling parental behavior that limits an infant's ability to develop a sense of efficacy or autonomy and would include, for example, a parent interrupting a child's natural exploration. For example, a new father, Jake, was playing with his baby, Kirby, with some new toys, and Kirby attempted to pick up a block and explore the shape. Jake took his son's hand and moved it to fit the block into its proper bin. He proceeded to hold his child's hand and pick up each block to put in the box. Jake was directing all the child's behavior and allowing for little exploration or free play. These types of father-child interactions were coded as high on intrusiveness. Finally, *stimulation of cognitive development* refers to the ways in which parents help to set up or structure a child's learning. Highly stimulating interactions occur when parents engage with their babies by labeling the child's experiences, reinforcing the child's attempts at mastery, and supporting their efforts to try new things. We used these four coding categories to measure parenting quality and understand patterns in the parent-child play episodes.

At the outset I was skeptical about using short, potentially awkward, videotaped interactions of parents playing with their infants and children as a means of assessing parenting. Would I want my own parenting to be evaluated this way? To test it out, my husband and I took part in the procedure. My students came to our home and taped us interacting with our children, who were two, six, and ten years old at the time. It felt uncomfortable and awkward at first, but once we started interacting with our children, the camera and the students became less visible. Sure, we were trying to put our best foot forward—trying to be engaging, fun, and supportive parents—but we were still being us. As it turned out, parents in our project had similar reactions to the procedure. When they started to interact with their babies and children in front of the camera, we were able to see a wide range of behaviors. Even if we assume that we were seeing them on their best behavior, there was still a wide variety in what those behaviors looked like.

## Work and Parenting Quality

My main question was simple: How were parents' work experiences related to the quality of their interactions with their babies? In pursuit of an answer, we recorded parent-child interactions approximately one month after parents had returned to work (when infants were about four months old), and again about one year after birth. We also had tremendous amounts of information about all aspects of parents' jobs, including work, schedules, hours, autonomy, and relationships. Our task was straightforward—examine how mothers' and fathers' experiences at work were connected to the quality of their interactions with their infants. We wanted to know, for example, if a father's autonomy at work was related to more responsive and engaged parenting at home, or if a mother's stress or sense of urgency at work related to less sensitive interactions with their infants. In short, is work directly related to parenting quality? As I noted earlier, however, it may be the case that, rather than directly affecting the quality of parenting, the effect of work is mediated through the parent in some way. Specifically, it may be that poor work conditions result in poor parental well-being (e.g., depression), and poor parental well-being relates to poorer parenting. Thus, we also set out to investigate whether parents' well-being provides the link between experiences on the job and parenting quality.

The connections between work and parenting, we discovered, differed for mothers and fathers, so I describe these findings separately. Turning first to mothers' experiences, we found that mothers who reported more job urgency and pressure at work were more responsive and sensitive with their infants. Our initial hunch had been that job pressure would be related to poorer parenting, so this result surprised us. Why did mothers who reported greater pressure at work engage in more sensitive parenting? As we dug a bit deeper, the explanation became clear. It was only in the cases where mothers reported high job satisfaction, in addition to high urgency at work, that they engaged in more positive parenting. When mothers reported high urgency in jobs but low job satisfaction, we observed less sensitive parenting, as we'd initially expected. In retrospect, this outcome makes sense. Job pressure is not always a bad thing—in fact pressure to finish a job on time and get it done correctly can be more stimulating than a job where time drags by, especially if you like your work. Mariana, who worked as a short-order cook at a large family-style restaurant, described just such a situation. "I love it when work is busy, and we work as team, and we get it done. It is like a well-oiled machine, orders in, cook, orders out. We are rolling."

Mothers' sense of self-direction and autonomy at work also mattered for parenting, but in an indirect way. Job autonomy contributed to mothers' overall sense of control in their lives, and it was this more generalized sense of control that was related to more sensitive parenting. What is meant by a generalized sense of control? In the psychological literature, this generalized sense of control is referred to as the "locus of control." An external locus of control involves the belief that one is helpless—that one's successes and failures are not within one's control. An internal locus of control, on the other hand, attributes successes and failures to one's own efforts. It turns out that having some autonomy and a sense of self-direction at work is related to workers having a greater internal locus of control in life, which is, in turn, linked to more sensitive parenting.

Erin, who worked as an employee service representative, provides a perfect example of how this process works. Erin experienced high autonomy at work: "I write my own schedule. It's very family oriented. . . . If I want to be able to take weekends off, there's an alternating weekends program, so you can do something like that . . . so I definitely feel that they do try to cater to the family needs and try to keep you close to home." For Erin, a high degree of control on her job led to a greater sense of control over her life; she saw herself as a key player in determining what happened in her life. Finally, Erin's greater sense of control was linked to her warm and sensitive interactions with her daughter. During her videotaped interaction, we saw Erin smiling, using soft gentle language, and touching her daughter continually. Erin let her daughter "take the lead" in her play, and Erin joined her in an engaging, nonintrusive way. Erin's positive work autonomy and overall sense of control in her life allowed her to be a responsive and warm mother.

We also found that, especially for mothers, having a supportive supervisor was related to a greater sense of control over one's life. When supervisors understood mothers' work-family challenges and provided flexibility and support, mothers reported a greater sense of overall control in their lives, which, in turn, led to more sensitive parenting with their infants. Mona's experience highlights this process. She worked as a receptionist at a hair salon, where her supervisor offered significant support: "Actually, it's [her workplace is] very responsive because I know that I've had to leave work because my son got sick. I told my manager I got to go 'cause my son is sick. . . . She was like, 'Bye.' I told her I felt bad, I told her I would try to make up the hours, and she was like, 'Bye.' She just didn't give it a second thought.

She's just like, 'Your kids come first.'" Not only did this lead Mona to develop tremendous loyalty to her supervisor, but it also translated into Mona feeling a greater sense of control in her life, which ultimately affected her ability to be a responsive and warm parent.

Lorna, who worked at Dunkin' Donuts, described the opposite experience. "I had to call out of work for my daughter because she was sick, and the next day I came in, and he [her supervisor] was like, 'You need to bring me a letter from the day care saying she wasn't there.' That was the day he sent me home. And it's funny because I'm the only one who has a small child who works there, and I'm the only one who needs to bring a notice? I mean, I'm a single parent; that should be excuse enough. He's not fair at all. Like I said, he's trying to make me quit, and it's not going to happen." Lorna clearly had little autonomy at work, and she felt her life was controlled by external sources, which related to her being less sensitive and more withdrawn with her daughter, Leah. What did these interactions between Lorna and Leah look like? During one interaction sequence, we asked Lorna to play with Leah using a new rattle that we gave her. As they started to play, Lorna began to continuously shake the rattle in Leah's face. The shaking was loud and constant. Leah started to get overwhelmed by the stimulation of the shaking rattle, and she turned her head from one side to another, seeking relief. Instead of letting Leah recover and return to play when she was ready, Lorna moved the rattle from side to side, keeping it in front of the baby's face and continuing to shake it. This lack of sensitivity to Leah's cues reflects a more intrusive and overcontrolling parenting style on Lorna's part. There were also times later in the play sequence where Lorna displayed more disengaged and distracted behavior, such as watching TV or checking her phone while playing with the baby.

In sum, in the early months of parenthood, mothers' autonomy at work and sense of control was related to more responsive and sensitive parenting styles. At the opposite end of the continuum, mothers with little job autonomy and who believed that they were powerless to external forces, such as chance, fate, or powerful others, displayed less skilled parenting styles. In the stories provided above, "powerful others," such as supervisors, had a tremendous ability either to exert external control over their workers or to support individual efficacy and autonomy in their workers, a key process whereby work experiences are transmitted to children.

At the one-year mark, we went back and videotaped parents with their infants again. We did this for a couple of reasons. First, we expected that, after a year, parents and children would have adjusted to the rhythms of life; routines like eating, sleeping, and child care would be well established. Moreover, by one year out, most children are sleeping through the night and have adjusted to a fairly regular, daily routine. Life for the parents might be easier. Second, as the children were more developed, we could observe a different type of interaction, in which babies could engage with toys and with their parents in a more proactive way. In order to see how parents supported their children's play, we laid out a large red blanket and spread out some new toys with which the child could play. We asked Mom, and then Dad, to sit with the child on the blanket and play with their child as they normally would for fifteen minutes. As before, these recordings were used to assess the quality of the parenting that we observed.

With respect to the relationship between work conditions and parenting, we found a similar, but not identical, pattern of results to those we observed at four months. First, a new finding emerged related to hours of employment. The more hours that mothers worked, the more responsive they were with their one-year-old babies. Although this result may seem counterintuitive, it is in line with other research[16] that shows that working full-time is protective for low-income mothers and results in better parenting. Full-time work provides resources and stability to the family that alleviates stress and allows mothers to be more engaged with their children.

For example, Janissa's experience made clear the importance of knowing that you are guaranteed a set number of hours per week at your job. When we first met Janissa, she worked at a large hotel in housekeeping, where her hours and income fluctuated both weekly and by the season. When we interviewed her later, she had changed jobs and worked at a car rental company with set, full-time hours. "In my past job, sometimes I would get sent home early or told not to come in at all, and I wouldn't get paid. I never knew how much I would make week to week. Now I get my forty hours, and it is set and good." A stable, full-time job, which brings a regular paycheck and a predictable schedule, makes it easier to be a responsive and caring parent—an important theme, which I will revisit when addressing the implications of our research for policy and action.

Looking beyond hours worked, we explored whether mothers' experiences of autonomy and job urgency were related to their interactions with their one-year-olds. We found few direct connections between mothers' work conditions and parenting: for example, greater urgency at work and more autonomy on the job were unrelated to how sensitive or responsive mothers were with their year-old babies. However, we discovered important indirect connections between work and parenting, which involved mothers' mental health.

Mothers with less autonomy on the job reported more anxiety and more depressive symptoms, what we refer to as psychological distress. In turn, greater mental distress was associated with less

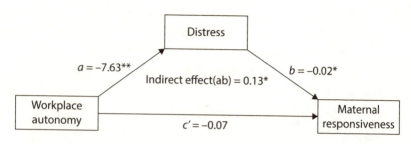

FIGURE 8. Mothers' work autonomy predicting psychological distress and parenting.

*Note*: Mediation Model: Work Autonomy and Responsiveness; $^*p < .05$; $^{**}p < .01$; $c'$ = direct effect from $a$ (work) to $c$ (parenting quality).

*Source*: Herman, R. J., and Perry-Jenkins, M. (2020). "Low-Wage Work Conditions and Mother-Infant Interaction Quality Across the Transition to Parenthood." *Journal of Child and Family Studies*, 29(12), 3552–3564. https://doi-org.silk.library.umass.edu/10.1007/s10826-020-01809-y.

sensitive parenting. This is illustrated in figure 8: the direct path between work autonomy and maternal responsiveness (path $c$) was not statistically significant, meaning work had no direct effect on parenting. But the mediated path—the path from work to maternal distress (path $a$), and from maternal distress to responsiveness (path $b$)—was significant. Less autonomy at work led to greater overall distress (i.e., more depression and anxiety), and this distress led to less responsive and sensitive parenting.

In sum, mothers' work experiences mattered for the quality of their parenting. With very young infants, a lack of job autonomy led mothers to report a more generalized lack of control and efficacy in their life, which resulted in a decline in parenting quality. As time progressed, we continued to see mediated processes linking work and parenting, in which poor work conditions led to poor mental health, and poor mental health led to poor parenting. As our findings demonstrate, the "long arm of a job" often reaches into family life.[17]

## What about the Fathers?

Thus far, the findings I have reported have been all about mothers, but for some families that's only half of the story. What about fathers? Does work have similar effects on fathers' abilities to be engaged and sensitive parents? To address this question, we asked fathers to participate in our parent-child interaction activities with their four-month-old and one-year-old babies. Many fathers (and many more fathers than mothers) were uncomfortable with the idea of being recording playing with their babies. When babies were about four months old, only forty-one fathers agreed to participate in the videotaped parent-infant interactions. Fathers often declined, saying they would "feel silly" or "under a microscope." However, as fathers came to trust us, more agreed to participate, and by the time the child was one year old, seventy-two fathers participated in the activity. Below I report the findings from this latter period, since we were better able to detect significant differences with a larger sample size, although similar trends emerged with the smaller group during the earlier period.

As with mothers, fathers' work conditions mattered for their parenting. Looking first at the structural conditions of fathers' jobs, like hours and schedules, we uncovered some interesting results.[18] Fathers with higher incomes and more stable and predictable work schedules displayed more sensitive and responsive parenting. Not only was there a direct link between these work factors and parenting quality, but we also found a more complex pattern: fathers with higher income and more stable job schedules were less anxious and depressed, which, in turn, was linked to more responsive parenting behavior. The opposite was also true. Lower incomes and unstable work schedules were a risk factor for fathers' well-being and for the quality of their parenting.

Unlike our results for mothers, we also found a direct link between work conditions and parenting for fathers. Specifically, fathers who reported more control and autonomy at work exhibited less intrusive parenting behaviors with their one-year-olds. We can only surmise about how this more direct process might work. It may be that when fathers are given more autonomy and control on the job, they internalize the value of autonomy, which they transmit to their child. Alternatively, perhaps when fathers lack control at work, they may make up for it by exerting control at home.

Jerome's story highlights how poor work conditions can affect parenting. In his interview, Jerome told us that parenting was "different than I thought. It's a lot tougher than I thought. You know, juggling everything as far as coming home from work and possibly taking care of the baby if Jen [his wife] has to do something. Sometimes you are tired, and sometimes you feel like you can't fill all his needs. He's raring to go, and you're tired you know." We also witnessed the challenges that Jerome described. On the day we observed Jerome, he had been at work all day. He worked for a package delivery company, and the Christmas holidays were approaching, so work was incredibly busy. His supervisor kept adding extra hours and shifts, which he could not decline since it was mandatory overtime. He reported little autonomy at work and very high time urgency. During the parent-child interaction component of the interview, Jerome appeared to be completely disengaged. As the baby began to grab different toys and throw them, Jerome sharply said "no." He kept the baby "corralled" on the blanket but made little effort to match his gaze, support his exploration, or simply smile and engage. Jerome might have just been having a bad day—we all have bad days—but when those days are repeated again and again, over weeks and months during the first year of life, children are likely to bear the brunt of those poor work conditions. Jerome also described having a "short fuse" at times with his son. "He [the baby] might do something wrong, and you hold back, you try not to get upset at him because you know he's one year old, and he doesn't know what he's doing. He dumps something over or something. I kind of get upset inside but try not to let him see it." As we have seen, stressed and disempowered parents struggle to control these daily parenting frustrations.

We all know it takes tremendous patience to care for infants. Logan, a package delivery worker, described the challenge aptly. "It is hard after a long day. I usually just get frustrated with him [his son] if he's, you know, he's screaming for no reason. Or if he obviously has a reason, but we have no idea—it's unknown to us, then I get really upset. I just go in the other room sometimes, lay on the bed." Another dad, talking about coming home after a long ten-hour day at work acknowledged, "I should do more. Dressing her. Bathe her. I need a little more patience."

Others, however described coming home to their child as relaxing, a time to destress. Dean said, "I walk in the door, and everything melts away. She gives me a big smile, and all feels right again." Mason actually noticed the ways his work affected his time with his baby girl, Mina. "On those long days, where the boss is yelling and everyone's pissed off, all I want to do is come home to quiet. I probably let her watch too much TV then. On my good days, I come home ready to roll. We take a walk, play around. I am better."

## Good Work, Better Parents

Work conditions matter for new parents and their children. Facilitating a supportive, engaging, and stimulating work environment for parents employed in low-wage work can support optimal caregiving. Parents told us exactly what a supportive work environment looked like: supervisors offer some flexibility in hours or schedules and give workers some say in how they get their work done or some control over daily tasks. Supervisors who solicit workers' input into how work can be accomplished better or faster not only create more autonomy for their workers; they also create more invested workers. Providing workers with some level of control in managing their hours, and some flexibility when they have a sick child or child-care issues, goes a long way to ease stress and, in the case of new, young parents, enhances the quality of their parenting. Our results also suggest that stressful, fast-paced work environments are not necessarily bad for working parents, so long as they are coupled with supportive supervisors and job satisfaction.

Earlier in this chapter, I shared Lorna's story. She worked at Dunkin' Donuts and felt unfairly targeted by her boss because she was a parent; she reported low autonomy at work and high time urgency. When we went back for her one-year interview, Lorna's situation had changed considerably. "I quit that lousy job. My supervisor was out to get me." Lorna had a new job working at a discount clothing store. "My boss is great. She lets me organize clothes, put together outfits to display. She is a mom too and totally gets it." She described her schedule as "a little nutty, but if I put in a request or need to switch shifts, it is all good." She received good discounts on clothes, which she proved to me by showing off her daughter's new outfit. Not only did Lorna feel happier with work, but she described being a happier mom. "It was not good when I came home all bitter and angry with my boss. I was in a bad temper a lot. I think I am more even now, calmer."

Parents often talked about work making them "steadier," "calmer," and "a better person," as well as "exhausted," "frustrated," and "angry." These feelings don't disappear when parents leave the job: they come home with those emotions, which shape the energy, warmth, and sensitivity they bring to their babies. A parent's consistent exposure to stressful, unsupportive, boring, and overcontrolled work settings is often transported home by tired, frustrated, and sometimes angry parents, which can have a devastating effect on family interactions. The upside is that the opposite is true as well. Feeling valued, energized, and even challenged at work can enhance the well-being and efficacy of a new parent and result in sensitive, warm, and engaged parenting. As one young mother perceptively described the importance of work: "My job is a part of me; it affects me and my mental health; it affects my husband and my kids; how could it not? When work is bad, I know I am grouchy, impatient. When it's good we good, when it's not . . . watch out."

# CHAPTER 6

# "I Just Want Him to Have a Good Start in Life"

### *Work and Child Development*

When I first met Melody, she was working as a shift supervisor at a coffee shop in the lobby of a large downtown hotel. Melody reported having "good fun" with her employees; she liked her customers and, in general, enjoyed "running the morning show." TJ, her fiancé, was working as a line cook at a local restaurant and also liked his job. The restaurant, located in the heart of the city, always had a steady flow of customers, and TJ enjoyed the bustling atmosphere because it made the time pass quickly. He described himself as more of a quiet guy: "I keep my head down and stay out of trouble." Both Melody and TJ had been working at their current jobs since graduating high school four years earlier and, perhaps surprisingly, reported having fairly high levels of autonomy at work. They were also both thrilled about the upcoming birth of their baby girl, although the pregnancy had been unexpected, and they had some concerns about being stretched financially. As TJ noted, "I am not sure we would ever really be ready; parenthood ain't cheap." They were busily preparing for the big transition, and one corner of their living room was piled high with gifts from their recent baby shower, including a swing, a stroller, a portable crib, and diapers.

Not long after our first interview, Melody gave birth to a healthy baby girl, Alexis. TJ had taken a week off after the birth, and Melody was in the middle of her eleven-week parental leave when we next spoke. During the interview it became clear that Melody was not happy about the thought of returning to work in five short weeks, but she knew they needed the money. Melody repeatedly expressed concerns about putting her daughter in day care, and how doing so might negatively affect her well-being and development. "You just don't know what goes on at those places. I had one friend who had a woman take care of her baby, and she had six other kids. . . . How can you take care of an infant with six other little ones around? That can't be good for their development." TJ expressed similar concerns about day care: "You just don't know what is going on there." Despite these concerns, the couple currently had a plan to place Alexis in a nearby family day-care home. About two weeks after our second interview, however, Melody contacted me to let me know that her mother, who had just been laid off, had volunteered to babysit Alexis. Partly as a result of this turn of events, Melody's transition back to work went quite well. "Oh, I am very satisfied. Work is good, and I have my mom; I just don't think that there can be anybody better to watch her than my mom. She is very attentive to her, and concerned about her. She spends a lot of time with her, and I think she is the best." Melody explained that she didn't want her work outside of the home to have a negative effect on her baby, but since her mother was helping out, she was no longer worried that it would.

While Melody's primary concern about the impact of her work on Alexis involved reliance on day care, as I have already shown there are several ways in which parents' work can directly or indirectly affect their child's development. For example, in describing her workplace, Melody talked about the sense of comradery among her coworkers. "We go out for drinks together, and they even had a baby shower for me." She also described the ways that work made her feel. "I guess I just like my job. I like talking with people, starting their day off right. I am a social being, so it is good for me to get out around other people. I am sure it makes me a better person." When I asked her to explain what she meant by that last statement, Melody replied, "You know, it just makes me feel productive and like I am contributing or something." From Melody's descriptions, I suspected that her work did, in fact, make her a better person, by giving her an opportunity to have friendships, develop confidence, and feel like she was making a positive impact on the world. I wanted to know if one of these positive work experiences might be having an impact on her baby girl. Would Melody and TJ's positive work experiences ultimately result in better developmental outcomes for their daughter?

I was able to address this question because our study followed families for several years, from birth through the first grade. When I went back to visit Melody and TJ five years later, Alexis greeted us at the door with a crown on her head and adorned in a pink princess gown. A chatty and outgoing little girl, she had just entered the first grade. I settled down to talk with Melody about how things were going, especially with regard to managing work and parenthood, and it was obvious that life had become much easier as Alexis had aged. "She goes to school now, and she is doing so well. She is a great kid and so smart; she got a good start, and it paid off." In Melody's mind, that good start involved loving care from Grandma. Although good child care was probably part of the explanation for Alexis's success, I suspected there was more to the story. In particular, I believed that an important piece of the puzzle was related to her parents' work experiences. Do positive job conditions, such as those Melody and TJ described, during that first, important year of a child's life predict better developmental outcomes for children? Conversely, do long hours, stressful work conditions, or unsupportive supervisors have negative long-term effects on children's social and emotional development?

In this chapter I dig into these questions and show that, in fact, parents' work experiences during their child's first year of life have significant implications for their child's development years down the road. In the previous chapter, I described the ways in which work, for better or worse, spills into home life. This chapter builds on that research by presenting the long-term consequences of this spillover for children's development. I first describe what our data revealed about the connections between work, parenting, and children's social and emotional outcomes, and then I illustrate these processes by drawing on stories from the families in our study.

## Some Background on Parents' Jobs and Children's Lives

Sociological scholars have argued that one way in which work affects parents, and parenting, is by shaping beliefs and values. Parents tend to adopt the values that are reinforced at work, and these values inform their parenting behaviors.[1] For example, if a job requires strict adherence to rules, little creativity, and a lack of control or autonomy, these same values are reflected at home through more controlling and rigid parenting styles—styles that are linked to poorer child outcomes. On the other hand, if one is rewarded at work for thinking "outside of the box," "pushing the boundaries," and coming up with new ideas, these same values of creativity and freethinking are reinforced at home.

An extensive literature in developmental psychology points to the importance of the early parent-child relationship in shaping children's socioemotional and cognitive development.[2] [3] Parents create a secure base for early infant development by providing support, teaching, and scaffolding to enrich social relationships and cognitive development. Under certain conditions, the timing and intensity of parental work during a child's first year of life have been shown to hold important consequences for children. For example, in the largest study of parents' work, child care, and early child development ever completed in the United States, work-family scholars Jeane Brooks-Gunn, Wen-Jun Han, and Jane Waldfogel found that full-time maternal employment during the first twelve months of life was associated with lower cognitive scores for children at 3 years, 4.5 years, and first grade. Although the pattern was consistent and statistically significant, these associations were small.[4] Part-time employment did not produce similar results. Moreover, no associations emerged between early maternal work and children's social and emotional outcomes. In this study, however, there were no data assessing parents' satisfaction, stress, or autonomy on the job, conditions that may be as important, if not more important, than hours and schedules.

A recent review of over sixty studies that explored the relationship between maternal employment and children's development reached more limited conclusions. With few exceptions, this review found that "early employment was not significantly associated with later achievement," depressive symptoms, or behavior problems in children.[5] However, they also found that these results varied across social classes. Mothers' employment in the first year of life had modest but beneficial effects on children's outcomes in low-income families, but slightly more negative effects for children in higher-income families. Two important points emerge from this work. First, the cost and benefits of maternal employment differ by socioeconomic status. Specifically, for low-income workers, where jobs bring economic stability and financial resources, the positive effects of income may outweigh the potentially negative effects of decreased maternal attention.[6][7][8] In wealthier families, no such benefit exists. Second, the effects of parental employment during the first year of a child's life and those of parental employment during later years may hold different implications for children's development. We know little about the cumulative effects of parental employment on children over time.

As I have mentioned previously, work-family researchers have devoted too little attention to the question of how fathers' employment relates to the lives of their children. Sociologist Katherine Gerson argues that the current culture of fatherhood calls for men to be both providers and equal partners in parenting,[9] and recent time-use data indicate that fathers engage in more "solo" and routine care when mothers are employed,[10] yet we know surprisingly little about how fathers' employment is related to the development of their children. One of the only studies to examine the relationship between fathers' work conditions and infant care found that low-income fathers who have more supportive supervisors at work exhibited more sensitive parenting behaviors.[11] However, significantly more research needs to be conducted to understand work-family relationships for fathers, especially during the transition to fatherhood, a time when child-care and involvement patterns are just being established. As fathers take on greater child responsibilities than ever before (though still not equal to mothers'), characteristics of their work are likely to affect their children and merit investigation.

What aspects of parents' work matters most for children's development? Is it parents' work hours, job stress, relationships with supervisors or coworkers, having a sense of control or autonomy, involvement in complex tasks, or schedules and flexibility? Recent research has found that jobs that provide self-direction and autonomy often involve problem solving and decision making, which translates to higher levels of occupational complexity. There is, moreover, convincing evidence that parents' occupational complexity has long-term, positive effects on children. One study, which focused on mothers who started new jobs with little complexity, found that the quality of the home environment provided to their children tended to decline over time.[12] In a more recent study, sociologists Ayse Yetis-Bayraktar, Michelle Budig, and Donald Tomaskovic-Devey examined the relationship between mothers' occupational complexity and the academic achievement of their preadolescent children.[13] They discovered that job complexity was associated with more autonomy, and that mothers who reported more autonomy during the first three years of the child's life had children with better academic outcomes years later. Thus, there is some evidence that children's long-term development is affected by aspects of parents' work early in life. However, existing research has focused almost exclusively on mothers' work and has focused far more attention on hours and schedules than on workplace conditions and policies.

## Parents' Work Experiences Matter for Kids

In order to understand whether parents' job experiences affected their children's long-term developmental outcomes, we examined whether mothers' and fathers' reports of job autonomy during the first year of their child's life predicted positive outcomes (social skills) and negative outcomes (behavior problems) when the child was entering the first grade. We relied on mothers', fathers', and teachers' reports of children's behavior, which allowed us to capture their behavior both at home and at school. The previous chapter emphasized how parents' jobs affected their sensitivity and responsiveness toward their infants. As the children in our project grew older, I continued to be interested in how conditions of parents' work could have a direct effect on children's development, but I also wanted to examine how work conditions affected children's development via parenting quality.

To capture a range of different parenting behaviors, we focused on two specific types of parenting that could serve as mechanisms connecting parents' work to child development. The first was called *overreactive parenting*, which refers to parents' inability to regulate their own emotions when interacting with their child; overreactive parents are often quick to anger and judgment. We reasoned that jobs in which parents have little control or self-direction may be frustrating and draining and, therefore, would leave less energy for effective parenting and produce, perhaps, more incidences of overreaction. As an example, Wes, who worked as a short-order cook at a busy breakfast place, talked about feeling disrespected and stressed at work: "My boss treats me like a two-year-old." He also described coming home to demanding and disrespectful children and "losing it" with them: "Yeah, I overreact to the littlest things sometimes. The little one spilled a whole gallon of milk on the floor, and I lost it. I felt kind of bad. It all just gets to you sometimes."

The second type of parenting behavior on which we focused was called *parent engagement*, which included activities like having a friendly talk with one's child, playing games, or doing other fun things together. Based on our findings with infants, we thought that autonomy at work would enhance parents' abilities to engage at home with their older children. Eliza's experiences in her job as a bill collector for a large insurance company illustrates how this might work. Her supervisor organized a morning workshop during which employees were taught how to use communication skills and problem-solving techniques with clients. They learned about active listening skills and "I" statements. Eliza thought the training was helpful and tried to use these skills with her six-year-old daughter, Skye. "They worked great. I listened to her, I reflected her ideas and feelings, and even though she is only six, she got it." This is one way in which employee autonomy and education at work rebounds to parent-child interactions at home and, if replicated over time, is likely to enhance child outcomes.[14]

Turning first to the results for mothers, we uncovered that the more job autonomy that mothers reported in the first year of their child's life, the fewer behavior problems their children exhibited in the first grade. Thus, mothers who experienced a sense of control and efficacy at work during the transition to parenthood had children with fewer behavior problems several years later. Beyond this direct link between mothers' work experience and children's behavior, there was also a more complex path connecting the two variables. Specifically, mothers with greater job autonomy were less likely to use harsh and overreactive parenting styles, which was associated with fewer child behavior problems. In other words, when work promotes autonomy and self-direction, mothers are better parents, which bodes well for children's development.

We examined these same relationships for fathers and found that, in fact, fathers work was equally important for children's development. When fathers reported having more job autonomy

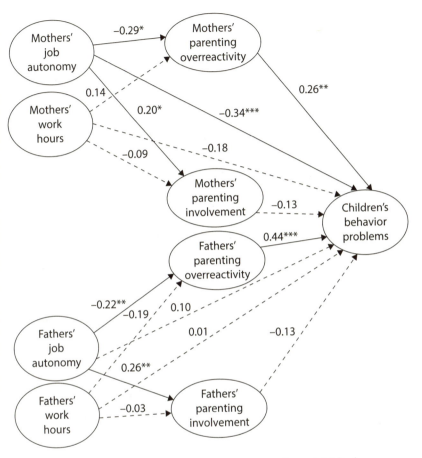

FIGURE 9. Parents' work conditions, parenting quality, and children's behavior problems.

*Note:* *p < .05; **p < .01; ***p < .001.

*Source:* Perry-Jenkins, M., Laws, H. B., Sayer, A., and Newkirk, K. (2020). "Parents' Work and Children's Development: A Longitudinal Investigation of Working-Class Families. *Journal of Family Psychology*, 34(3), 257–268. https://doi.org/10.1037/fam0000580.

during the first year of parenthood, they also engaged in more skilled and less overreactive parenting, which resulted in fewer behavior problems in their children. Low-income mothers and fathers who worked as hairdressers, laborers, certified nursing assistants, and bus drivers, and who reported having a sense of autonomy on the job during their child's first year of life, had six-year-olds with fewer behavior problems. These long-term effects point to the salience of the first year of life in setting the stage for both parents and children.

While figure 9 describes the relationship between parents' work and children's behavior problems, figure 10 describes the relationship between parents' work and a positive child outcome, namely, adaptive skills. Adaptive skills refer to a child's abilities to adapt to new situations, positively interact with their peers, and develop friendships. Much of the research on work and child development has been so hyperfocused on the possible negative effects of parents' employment that researchers have rarely looked for positive impacts that work might have on children. Our findings here were heartening.

For mothers, greater job autonomy during the child's first year of life was related to higher-quality parenting, namely, less overreactive parenting and greater parent involvement, which resulted in first graders with better social skills. Turning to fathers, the findings were equally compelling. As shown by the paths in the bottom half of figure 10, more autonomy at work was linked to less overreactive parenting and higher levels of parent involvement. In turn, higher-quality parenting by fathers was related to greater social skills in their first graders. These are some of the first data highlighting just how critical fathers' work may be to parenting and child development.

In sum, we found that mothers' and fathers' experiences of work during the first year of parenthood have long-term

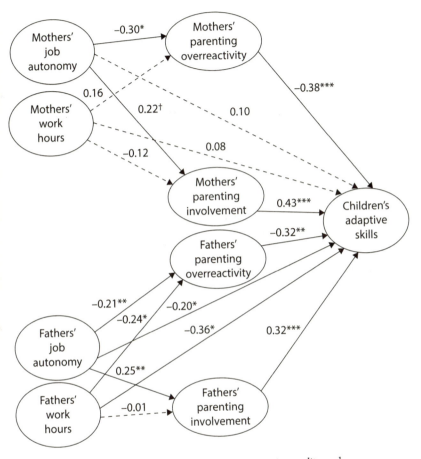

FIGURE 10. Parents' work conditions, parenting quality, and children's adaptive skills.

*Note:* *p < .05; **p < .01; ***p < .001.

*Source:* Perry-Jenkins, M., Laws, H. B., Sayer, A., and Newkirk, K. (2020). "Parents' Work and Children's Development: A Longitudinal Investigation of Working-Class Families. *Journal of Family Psychology,* 34(3), 257–268. https://doi.org/10.1037/fam0000580.

implications for both positive and negative developmental out-comes in their children. Without downplaying the significance of these findings, it is important to acknowledge that it is a long leap from experiences during the child's first year of life to their social development in the first grade, and that much else is going on during these early years. In the following section, I provide some examples and evidence for how these early work conditions may set the stage for later parenting behaviors and child outcomes.

## Parents' Work and Children's Development: Piecing Together the Puzzle

When we went back to interview our families six years later—by which time their "babies" had become first graders—much had changed. For many families, there were new siblings, new dogs, new jobs, new houses, and sometimes new partners. It was fun reentering these families' lives, and, for the most part, they seemed happy to see us. They were eager to talk about how life had changed since that first year and share with us the ups and downs they had experienced along the way. We also had the opportunity to talk with the children and learn a little about their lives.

During the interview, we asked parents to describe their child's personality, likes and dislikes, and achievements and struggles. As moms and dads described their children to us, I noticed that they almost never talked about their experiences during the first year of parenthood as shaping their child's be-havior and development. That first year was a distant memory. Yet we know that those early experiences have a unique and powerful effect on children. What was the best way to link what we knew about the experiences during that first year for our families with the information that parents were sharing with us about their child's development? I decided to work backward to try to understand how these processes might work. To do this, I identified children who were in the top 25 percent of social skills and the lowest 25 percent of behavior problems, as reported by parents and teachers; these were the children who were doing the best among our families. I also identified the opposite group, those children in the bottom 25 percent of social skills and top 25 percent of behavior problems, a group of children with more developmental challenges. After identifying these two groups, I went back to see what their parents' work lives had looked like during the first year of parenthood.

I was not surprised to see that Joshua, the six-year-old son of Carla and Cedric, fell into the well-functioning group. Carla and Cedric were a young African-American couple I had interviewed years earlier. At the first interview, Carla expressed concerns about balancing her job with parenthood. She worked as a staff assistant to a project manager at a local engineering firm and felt lucky to have this position with only a high school degree; as she explained, she had moved up in the ranks because of her organizational skills and strong work ethic. She loved the fast pace of her job, enjoyed interacting with clients, and felt valued by her boss. Cedric was a long-distance trucker who left home early Monday mornings and returned Friday afternoons, traveling all over the East Coast during the week. Both were extremely concerned about how Carla was going to manage caring for the baby while Cedric was away, and it appeared that they would be facing some serious work-family challenges when Carla returned to work.

After Joshua was born, the couple made some dramatic decisions. Cedric had "fallen in love with fatherhood" and worried that his work would make him an absent father. As he lamented,

"I am not about to miss out on my son's first steps because of some lousy job." Cedric quit his job and decided to go back to school to become a refrigeration technician. The job required only one year of training, offered good pay, and was in high demand. So Cedric found an interim job, as a maintenance worker at a nearby apartment complex, that he could do during the day and attended school in the evening. These changes required some sacrifices from both Carla and Cedric as they managed two jobs, a significant decline in family income, Cedric's return to school, and the care of a new child. But they both seemed determined to make it work, and the change ensured that Cedric would be living in the same house as Carla and Joshua during the week.

At the one-year interview, life was hectic but upbeat in their household. As Carla described the situation, "When I was growing, my mom ran a business out of our house; looking back, I don't think my mom gave us the quality time that I give to my child. She just tried to keep me busy watching her do her work. When I come home, I spend all my time with him [Josh] because I miss him so much. I really don't care what else happens around here. We try to clean when we can, we cook when we can. No more big meals, no more perfect house, and that's OK." Cedric was about halfway through his technician training program, and although he was busy, he felt like he was working toward a goal. "I am doing this for him [Josh] and us. I will have a job I am proud of."

I was excited to visit Carla, Cedric, and Joshua six years later to see how things had turned out. They still lived in the same home, and as we walked in the back door we were greeted by an adorable little boy, Joshua, wearing a superhero costume and waving a light-up shield. Carla was standing in the kitchen, holding a little girl on her hip and smiling broadly as Joshua showed off for us. Cedric welcomed us into the house, noting, "Well, as you can see, things have changed a bit since you were last here." Carla put Janelle, their three-year-old, down for a nap and went to talk with one of my graduate students in the kitchen, while Cedric and I stayed in the living room. Joshua went with another student of mine to play some games and answer questions about being a big brother. Cedric immediately let me know that he had completed his refrigeration technician degree and was doing well. He had his own truck and worked about fifty-five hours per week, making good money, especially with the overtime. He liked using his skills and enjoyed the freedom of having his own truck and clients. He proudly talked about being an involved father, coaching Joshua's T-ball team, and taking the kids fishing to give Carla a break. Carla was still at the engineering firm; as the firm grew, she had gained more responsibility and even supervised some staff. Joshua was doing well in school and had made plenty of friends. As Cedric described, "He is one high-energy kid, but he is a good kid. We got lucky with that one. Janelle too, she is a cutie." I suspect that luck did not have much to do with it. Carla and Cedric were engaged, attentive parents. Although they were juggling many balls, they were in control of their lives and felt proud of what they had accomplished.

Zena and Mark stood in stark contrast to Carla and Cedric. Their six-year-old daughter, Virginia, was facing serious emotional challenges. She cried on the way to school every day, and her teacher had contacted her parents numerous times to express concern about Virginia's lack of engagement and integration with the other children. Both her parents and her teacher reported that she had poor social skills and trouble making friends. When I went back to look at Mark and Zena's lives during their first year of parenthood, I found that their road had been a hard one. Mark had worked 11 p.m. to 7 a.m., five days each week, as a night guard at a large insurance company, a job he found boring, lonely, and unfulfilling. He made extra money working under the table for his cousin's car detailing business about three days each week. Zena worked full-time at a laundry shop, doing washes, folding clothes, and packing up packages for customers. "It is not a great job. I hate touching other people's dirty clothes. My boss is a pain; he just pushes and pushes to get more done faster." Zena and Mark were unhappy at work, and their opposite schedules led to fairly solitary lives, with little time for each other. After Virginia was born, they used opposite shift schedules to manage baby care, which Mark hated. "I am up all night and have to take care of her during the day. My mom comes over sometimes, so I can sleep, but I usually have to wait for Zena to come home and sleep from like three to eight before I go into work." Mark felt like he was always trying to get the baby to sleep, instead of playing with her, so he could get some sleep. He felt bad about the situation, but he was also completely exhausted. "I know my temper is shorter because I am just walking around on no sleep. I just don't have a lot of patience these days." Both Zena and Mark shared that they fought frequently during that first year, and loudly enough that their neighbors had called the police a few times. They fought about money, child care, and in-laws. Both felt that the pressure of work and parenthood was relentless, without any release. Years later, not much had changed.

Looking back at characteristics of Mark's and Zena's jobs, both reported low autonomy, low supervisor support, and high job pressure across the first year of Virginia's life. While one could argue that this couple faced a number of challenges, any one of which might have led to their little girl's adjustment problem, our data point to parents' early work conditions as one key factor contributing to their daughter's behavior problems. This is an important finding, in part, because current family research and policy rarely considers parents' work a significant contributor to child development. Often, interventions and supports for new parents focus on the parents themselves by, for example, teaching them parenting skills. While there is nothing inherently wrong with teaching skills to new parents, this approach overlooks how stressors, like unpredictable work schedules or demanding supervisors, interfere with good parenting—even when parents know what good parenting looks like. Many of the parents in our study, like Mark, were well aware of the moments when they were falling short. The message from our research is clear: challenging work conditions make it hard to be warm and sensitive parents, while positive conditions enhance the quality of parenting. One of the best things society could do to support new parents and their children would be to focus more attention on the workplace, a theme to which I will return in the final chapter.

## Work, Parenting, and Child Development over Time

During these first-grade follow-up interviews, we were interested to learn how the demands of work and family life had changed as the children grew older and their schedules became more complicated. Our interview with Crystal and Zach, a White couple with three children under the age of six, highlighted the challenges that many couples faced during this stage of family life. Crystal worked at an insurance call center, the same job she had five years earlier when she was pregnant with Chavon, her oldest daughter. She had been promoted to shift supervisor, a position that brought "lots of headaches" but more money. Zach was also in the same job, working as an assembly specialist at a local gun factory. He had just transferred to the day shift, after working for five years on the evening shift (3 p.m. to 11 p.m.). He was happier but felt that working days was more stressful because there were "too many people to deal with during days." As we separated for our interviews, I sat down with Zach on the picnic table in the backyard, so he could have a smoke, and we started to talk about managing work and parenting. "I figured it'd be hard. I didn't think it would be this hard. . . . This was all planned; we planned our kids. Of course, throwing an extra kid in the mix really made it a lot harder, but I think we didn't really fully understand what we thought we were committing to. So, it's been hard. My wife is less supportive of my job than I expected her to be." I asked Zach what he meant, and he said that he had to take less overtime at the factory because Crystal felt like she was dealing with family responsibilities on her own. "I do it [overtime] because we need the money, but she doesn't seem to get that."

Zach went on to talk about parenting: "It's so much harder. You can plan and understand and know that it's going to be hard. To actually finally go through the tough bit, it's just, the act, the actually experience of it, it's almost like sometimes you can't get yourself emotionally psyched up to deal with it." The experience of parenting was harder than he had anticipated, a feeling that almost every parent in our study expressed in one way or another. No time to breathe, no time for yourself, "just work, kids, wife on an automatic cycle."

We found that parents who liked their jobs often talked about work as a respite, a place of refuge from the stress of a challenging child or toddler. Betsy talked about her time at the beauty salon, where she worked as a hairdresser, as her "moment to breathe." "Getting those kids out the door to day care and school is complete craziness. Finding shoes, getting some breakfast into them, stopping the fights. Work is nice and calm." Todd also saw work as the easier place to be. "She [his wife] thinks I work late sometimes or go in early just to avoid the insanity. . . . She is not wrong."

The most challenging times emerged when parents found little sustenance at either home or work. Parents in this situation were highly stressed, and many were depressed. They often felt trapped in their jobs because they simply could not afford to quit, and the effort to find a new job seemed overwhelming. Cassie worked in the bakery at the local food store. "My job is stressful, mainly because my boss is just all over me all the time. He rushes me and then gets mad if I mess something up, but I mess it up because of the pressure. No one likes him, but he is the manager's nephew, so he isn't going anywhere." When Cassie headed home for the day, she stepped out of one stressful situation and into another: "My two girls are like two wet cats together. They just fight and bicker and whine and cry. It just wears me down. And then I am so tired I just give in and give them whatever they want. I am not proud of it, but sometimes you got to do what you got to do. Tim doesn't get home until eleven, so it is all on me."

Older children also brought a different set of problems and issues from those that infants did—challenges that can affect parents' work. Chris, who worked as a mechanic, described the challenges he and his wife were facing with their six-year-old, Aaron. "I feel like we are good parents. But dealing with what he is learning at school and his behavior, especially right now, is a lot. He has no respect. It seems like he has no respect for us at all. We try to do a lot of good things for our kids that we both didn't get growing up, and he doesn't appreciate stuff like I thought he would." Aaron was often in trouble at school, where he refused to listen to his teacher and played the role of the class clown. Chris felt like he had made significant sacrifices for his family and Aaron, including stopping things about which he felt passionate. "You know, I used to be a volunteer fireman, a volunteer EMT; the policing and the emergency services, that's really my passion. And I've had to give up a lot of that. I feel guilty because my wife is home with my kids if I do that."

Gia, a member of the armed forces, was unexpectedly deployed for six months when her children were three and six years old. Her husband, Carlos, was left to care for the children while holding down his job with a security firm. Carlos went to his boss to see what they could do to help him out. As Carlos explained, "When my wife got deployed, I had one hundred hours of comp time on the books. And my boss allowed me to use that comp time as I needed to for the kids. I actually requested to come off the street and work inside for the months she was gone." He went on to describe how he was able to reshape his day to accommodate his family obligations. "I was on the 12 a.m. to 8 a.m. shift and had a babysitter sleep over with the kids. I took an hour every day during the week of comp time and left at seven instead of eight to go home and get the kids ready for school—and I walked them to school. This way here, I mean, I was always home for the kids when they got out of school, we always went to bed together, and then in the morning when they got up to go to school, I was home." Carlos was extremely grateful to his team leader and noted that although there were existing department policies and procedures, his supervisor devised new rules to accommodate his situation. Our interview with his six-year-old son, Rory, revealed a happy little boy who was coping well with his mother's absence. He talked about missing her, but she FaceTimed almost every day, and that worked for him. According to his teacher, Rory was excelling academically and displayed outstanding social skills. By focusing his attention on the children and shifting his work priorities, Carlos was able to overcome the challenge of Gia's deployment.

Not all workers, however, can rely on the generosity and creativity of their bosses to make these kinds of adjustments. Supervisors need to be given some discretion and training to support their workers in exceptional circumstances. Workers described many instances in which their supervisors "broke the rules" or "bypassed the rules" to help them out. How might work experiences change if supervisors were given the power to create a work environment that supported workers, offered some flexibility, and provided some self-direction and control? Based on what parents in our project described, this type of work environment could make a real difference for parents and children.

Our research points to ways in which parents' work experiences during the first year of a child's life hold important consequences for their later development. There are, of course, many other factors that need to be considered—including personality characteristics of parents and children, social support, siblings, extended kin, neighborhood, and schools. Our findings show that characteristics of low-income jobs are related to child outcomes, but those work conditions are also likely to be related to characteristics of the parents themselves (e.g., their gregariousness or shyness). Moreover, income is directly linked to the quality of schools that children attend, the safety of their neighborhoods, and the opportunities available to them. These complexities cannot be overlooked when trying to pinpoint the various causal mechanisms that influence a child's trajectory.

With that said, our data clearly show that parents' early work experiences are related to their children's development. This is significant and fills a gap in our understanding. Previously, parents' work was rarely considered a context that shapes children. There is an important message here: one way that society can support new parents, and ultimately the well-being of their children, is to provide good, stable work, where positive relationships can thrive and workers feel empowered.

# CHAPTER 7

# "Thriving or Surviving"

## How to Move Forward

According to recent figures released by the Bureau of Labor Statistics, low-wage jobs are not going to disappear anytime soon (see figure 11). Given that reality, I have attempted to highlight how different conditions of low-wage jobs—such as hours, schedule flexibility, leave policies, relationships at work, and autonomy on the job—shape parents' well-being, parenting quality, and, in turn, children's well-being. These findings are important, in part, because they convey an intimate picture of what life is like for many low-income, working families in America. They also provide an informed perspective from which to answer the practical question faced by academics, policy makers, employers, and many American families: what can be done to support low-income, working families?

A recent report by the National Women's Law Center (NWLC) proposed several interventions to protect low-wage workers, including: (1) increasing income and job security, (2) providing predictable and stable work hours, (3) granting more autonomy over work schedules, (4) expanding access to high-quality child care, (5) providing more paid time off, sick time, and paid

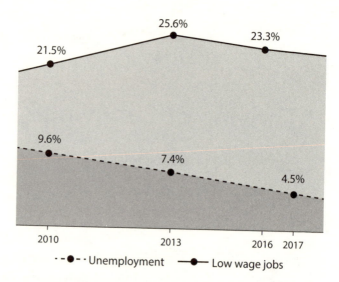

FIGURE 11. Unemployment falling, low-wage jobs remaining high.
*Source*: Bureau of Labor Statistics and Occupational
Employment Statistics.

family leave benefits, and (6) giving workers a voice in improving conditions of employment.[1] Many of these suggestions focus on issues related to time, a precious commodity for all the families with whom we talked. They needed more time to sleep, more time to work, more time to care for babies, more time to connect with one's partner, or simply more time to be alone. Parents also needed predictability in their time, meaning consistent and set hours, and they expressed the need for some control over their time, such as the ability to plan for last-minute doctor appointments. Policies that address issues such as parental leave, sick time, personal time, flexibility, and predictability are critical to improving the lives of low-income families. This has been a resounding theme in many studies on low-wage workers, so it was not surprising that these issues were raised again and again by the families we interviewed. These are also issues that a variety of policy initiatives across the country are beginning to address, and I will discuss some of these same issues later in this chapter; however, I first want to focus on the idea of improving work conditions, a topic that I believe has received less attention from scholars and policy makers than it deserves.

The final intervention recommended by the NWLC report referenced above is to give "workers a voice in improving conditions of employment."[2] In policy efforts to support families by providing flexibility, predictability, and time away from work, the impact of spending forty hours (or more) per week "on the job" is often overlooked. The experiences that occur on the factory floor, in the nursing home, or on food service lines—day in and day out for most of one's adult life—affect workers' mental health, physical health, stress, and energy. These experiences also affect workers' abilities to be engaged and sensitive parents. The question of how to "create" low-wage jobs that provide autonomy, meaning, and support requires listening to the workers themselves and understanding what about their work matters to them. It requires letting go of narratives that describe low-wage workers only as victims, as individuals who are hopeless, powerless, beaten down, and in need of help. It requires that those with a platform or the power to advocate for change make certain that the proposed changes reflect workers' and parents' experiences and opinions.

As a researcher, I constantly remind myself to resist oversimplifying the stories I tell with the data. It is easy to fall into familiar narratives: that high-paying jobs are inherently better than low-wage jobs, that no one wants to stay in a low-wage job, or that no one enjoys a low-wage job. Such a simple view suggests that, for low-income workers, the transition to parenthood will inevitably be a time of stress and unhappiness. But as we found in our study, and as I have attempted to relay in this book, the experience of parenthood for low-wage workers is far from uniform. One story—my favorite from all my years interviewing parents, and which I share with my students every year when preparing them to go into the community to interview parents—provided me with an important reminder that there is no one story to tell about low-income, working families.

Brendon and Shawna lived in a tiny house, just beyond the city limits. We first met them on a beautiful, crisp fall day, and as we walked up their driveway to the side door, where we had been told to enter, I was startled to see a dead deer hanging from a tree in the yard. In the driveway, there was a huge pickup truck with a full gun rack on the back of the cab and hunting gear laid neatly in the truck bed. My student and I glanced at each other, working hard to hide our distaste for guns and dead animals. We knocked and heard someone call, "Come in," so we opened the door. Within seconds a large black dog, who was clearly not happy with the strangers who had just entered his house, began to bark and snarl at us. Brendon walked in and yelled, "King, knock it off, get outside!" He opened the door and shoved the dog into the fenced-in yard. Brendon was a large man, well over six feet tall, with a large belly, full beard, and balding head. Shawna walked in quietly as we began to place our bags on the kitchen table. The difference in their manner and style was immediately apparent. Shawna was slight in stature and stooped a bit. She spoke softly, almost in a whisper, and seemed uncomfortable with the whole situation; she said hello and offered a weak handshake. Brendon, meanwhile, was explaining to us that King was harmless, and he hoped we weren't scared.

We sat down at the kitchen table, made our introductions, and explained the process a bit, as we always do. I suggested that we separate for the interviews, and Brendon said we could talk privately downstairs in his "man cave," while Shawna and my graduate student could remain upstairs at the kitchen table. I grabbed my bag and headed downstairs with Brendon. After my eyes adjusted to the faint light provided by the Bud Light sign over the bar, I took a seat on a low, sagging couch, pulled out my interview book, and peered around the room. There was a full bar with multiple neon beer signs and a large spout for a keg. A huge flat-screen TV hung on the opposite wall, surrounded by New England Patriots flags, shirts, and memorabilia. The wall at the end of the room was decorated with three sets of antlers, one full deer head, and a few old guns, which Brendon later told me were antiques given to him by his grandfather.

I began the interview already sure about what I would hear from Brendon on the subjects of pregnancy, parenthood, work, and his relationship with Shawna: he would tell me about the traditional roles of men and women, that his job was to provide, and her job was to take care of the home. He would talk about his buddies, hunting trips, and weekly Patriot game parties, none of which he would expect to change once the baby arrived. I didn't expect that he had spent much time thinking about fatherhood. But then the interview began. "Brendon," I asked, "how are you feeling about you and Shawna having a baby at this point? How are things going?" He paused for a long while and then said, "You know, I am not really sure how I feel, or should feel. I am excited. For me, probably for most men, you know, pregnancy is really a theory, you know?" Not the response I expected. "Can you tell me more?" I asked. "Well, a theory is an explanation for a phenomenon, right, so my wife and all the books I read tell me about what is supposed to happen, and what is happening in this pregnancy, and I must suspend judgment and believe that this is the case. I can never experience it firsthand. I guess it is hard for me to fully empathize with her. I have been writing about this in my journal." Brendon pointed to a cabinet below the flat-screen TV loaded with reams of notebooks, his journals. He pulled the most recent book out and read me a bit. "I am going to be a father. What does that mean? Who is this little being growing in my wife's body? Is it real? Everyone tells me what the baby is doing, how Shawna is feeling. . . . For me . . . it is all a bit of mystery. I accept all these explanations, but I can never really know. I will just have to meet this child to know it is real." Brendon went on to read me a few poems that he had written for his unborn child, which described the thoughts, the love, the confusion, and the momentousness of the event that was about to occur. I was overwhelmed. I asked Brendon if he had shared any of this writing or his thoughts with Shawna. He responded, "No, we don't talk about this stuff." The rest of my interview with Brendon highlighted his deep concerns about whether he would be a good father and his profound sense of fatherhood as a "calling." He also talked about being a good provider and the immense pressure he felt to be "a man." "Even if I want to be a good dad, I can't be that unless I bring home money first. Would you think I was a good dad if I didn't put a roof over my family's head?" I didn't answer. He went on, "But Shawna could not work and still be a good mother. Doesn't really seem fair. I am not blaming her or anything, but the rules are different, aren't they?" He was right. The rules are different. The same behaviors performed by mothers and fathers hold different meaning and different consequences.

On our ride home that day, my student and I compared notes. Shawna was a bit annoyed with Brendon because she didn't think that he was taking their impending parenthood seriously. She had no idea that he was downstairs writing poetry and deeply contemplating the changes about to occur to their family. This story is important to me because it illustrates how quickly, as a researcher, one can get into a rigid mind-set about what is happening for families during this critical transition. Despite what I tell my students when training them for these interviews—that "the parents are the experts," "our job is to listen and not judge," and "we want to give them a voice"—I had clearly developed a certain set of expectations about what I would hear, rather than staying open to the range of experiences. While Brendon held only a high school degree, he had a level of insight and curiosity about fatherhood that surpassed most. His story was uncommon, no doubt, but it was a story that it is easy to overlook when one begins to generalize about working-class families.

In what follows, I walk a fine line between summarizing important themes from research with low-income families and obscuring the richness of their individuality. I highlight what I see as some key "takeaway" messages that emerged from our work with the 360 families who shared their lives with us for a short time. I also propose some recommendations for policy makers, employers, and researchers for how they might alleviate the very real and unique challenges facing low-wage, working parents.

## "Twenty-Eight Hours in a Day Would Be Helpful": The Perspectives of Parents

Most of the couples we interviewed were busy before parenthood had even started. All were working full-time, some were going to school, some had other family responsibilities, and some worked multiple jobs. Their days were full. How does an already busy, dual-earner couple or working, single mother manage the new demands of infant care? According to most estimates, infant care increases parents' daily workload by about six to eight hours: feeding a newborn can take between five and six hours a day; changing countless diapers a day takes at least an additional hour; bathing, dressing, and soothing a child is easily an additional hour or two. In short, new parents are performing a second full-time job. Outside child care covers some of this additional labor, but the second shift kicks in the minute Mom or Dad arrives home from work. It is no surprise that time becomes the most precious commodity for parents with infants. Not only is there a shortage of time, but there is also a shortage of time during which parents feel in control. Parents can't plan on sleepless nights, colic, or illness. Parents can't plan for sick days or sick caregivers, yet many workplaces require advance notice for paid time off. On the work front, parents have little to say about schedules, flexibility, or the timing of their work tasks.

During interviews, we asked parents, "Have you thought of anything that might help you with the 'juggling act' of combining parenting and working?" What struck me most when talking to these young parents was their lack of attention to the ways that government or workplaces might ease their burdens. Few expressed any sense of entitlement to benefits or support. Instead of mentioning the possibility of paid leave, paid sick time, scheduling flexibility, or child-care benefits, they focused on things that they, themselves, could or should do differently. They repeatedly said things like "Maybe I should sleep less," or "I should be more organized" or "pray to God more." Even when we directly asked them to think about how their employer might be able to help them, the majority of our parents could not think of one way that their workplace could support them. When they did respond, they often provided nonspecific comments, like "Maybe they could give me more time" or "pay me more." A small percentage suggested that child-care support would be helpful, but only a handful mentioned paid family leave, despite having previously acknowledged in the interview the significant struggles they faced during the period immediately after their child's birth.

Why did so few parents identify policies that their employers could offer them? I think that many parents we interviewed saw social institutions, like workplaces or day-care settings, as completely immutable. Moreover, the idea that employers have a responsibility to support their employees was completely foreign to them. These parents saw their work-family challenges as a function of their own shortcomings, related to poor time management skills or lack of fortitude, rather than as the product of the social rules and institutions to which they were subject. These reactions were completely different from those I have heard from middle-class, professional workers or from skilled, union workers, neither of whom hesitate to list the ways their company's policies fall short.

It is also likely the case that some low-income workers simply don't trust government or employers to solve their problems, a suspicion that is often borne out of experience. For many low-income workers, the political and economic reality is that they lack the power to ask for more from their company, or from those who represent them. Perhaps the individualistic solutions they propose are based in that reality. Whatever the case, class differences matter in attempting to understand not only how parents interpret work-family challenges, but also the solutions they pose to solve them.

Thus, I believe that policy makers, employers, and researchers must continually solicit feedback from workers themselves about which policies and supports would be most important to them. Their voices matter. When given a chance to truly speak up, many workers I talked with, especially in conversation with their coworkers, were quite creative problem solvers. Once a policy is instituted, workers need to be consulted about the consequences of the policy. Did it help? Did it help some workers more than others? What else could be done? Often, when researchers evaluate the effectiveness of a new policy in the United States like the current paid leave policies popping up in states across the country, success is demonstrated by proving to employers or policy makers that the policy was cost-effective—that any expenses were offset by reduced turnover or gains in productivity. What if, instead (or at least in addition), researchers and policy makers measured success by a reduction in working parents' stress, or the improved well-being of parents and children? Or what about happiness? In a provocative study, sociologists Jennifer Glass, Robin Simon, and Matthew Andersson found that parents in the United States reported the lowest levels of happiness among the twenty-two OECD (Organisation for Economic Co-operation and Development) countries in their study. As parents almost always say about their children, "I just want them to be happy." Perhaps the time has come for the United States to say the same about parents.

## What Should Be Done?

Drawing on the research in this book, as well as policy experimentation by various states, let me offer four policy-oriented recommendations for how the United States might improve the lives of low-income, working parents.

*Offer a minimum of twelve weeks of paid leave for all new parents.* As the preceding pages of this book have made clear, new parents need time to adjust to their new circumstances, and most low-income parents lack the economic cushion necessary to take more than a few weeks of unpaid leave without experiencing significant financial strain. Currently, California, Hawaii, New Jersey, New York, Rhode Island, Washington, and Washington, DC, offer paid leave arrangements ranging from four to six weeks at 55 to 66 percent of pay to twelve weeks of pay. Washington state offers $250 per week for five weeks. New York is the first state to guarantee twelve weeks of paid leave. Slowly, steps are being taken, state by state. These efforts represent a starting point, but the efforts so far are small and inadequate. To be clear, I believe we should be advocating for longer leaves, at least six months. International data in countries where leaves are much longer, extending six to twelve months or even longer, show that longer leaves predict significantly better outcomes for mothers, fathers, and children.

*Personal time off (PTO) should not take the place of sick leave.* Many workplaces currently do not offer a stand-alone sick leave benefit but rather offer PTO that bundles vacation, sick, and personal time into one bank. The problem with this arrangement is that personal time off usually requires advance notice, and employees can be refused the time. In the worst-case scenarios, a sick employee can be denied PTO to stay home from work. As Juan described, "Personal time sounds good doesn't it? Problem is you have to plan for it, ask for it, and you can be told, flat out, No. How do I plan for a sick baby? How do I plan for no child care? At least with sick time, you call in as sick, and you don't get a black mark." When I have advocated for sick time policies in my own state, many legislators did not understand the hidden problems with personal time and the need for sick time benefits.

*Workers must have a voice in developing work-family solutions.* Although many workers tend to think of the workplace and employers as immutable and policies as set, deeper conversations about their own work settings often yield thoughtful, creative, and "doable" solutions. For example, Camila described how she and her coworkers volunteered to organize shift coverage, outside of the company software schedule, a month in advance as opposed to the old model that only gave two weeks' notice. "Our boss likes it because we are happy, he doesn't have to do it, and we can plan." Similarly, Leo went to the union to complain about getting penalized for taking personal time for his sick child and became involved in rewriting the union proposal. Leo was an exception, as fewer than 8 percent of workers in our study were in unionized jobs, but the lesson from his experience was clear: through the union, he became empowered to ask for what he was owed. One way that policy makers can support low-income, working parents is to enact policies that ensure workers have a greater voice in their workplaces by, for example, making it easier to organize. The recent Protecting the Right to Organize (PRO) Act, which passed through the US House but is unlikely to advance to the Senate, aims to empower workers to have a voice, address inequality, and organize for change.[3]

*Addressing the rigidity of mandatory overtime.* In the United States employers can force employees to work mandatory overtime according to the Fair Labor Standards Act. Employees must be paid time and a half for hours worked beyond the forty-hour workweek. Many parents I talked with wanted the overtime and needed the money. At the same time, however, the unpredictability of forced overtime created tremendous hardship for some families who needed to pick up their children from day care or relieve another parent so he or she could get to work. According to economists Lonnie Golden and Barbara Wiens-Tuers, mandatory overtime results in employees reporting lower job satisfaction, having less say at work (i.e., autonomy), and greater work-family interference.[4] Again, this is a place where management and workers could collaborate to develop workplace policies that could help to manage the predictability of when overtime is needed and organize a plan for which workers would be asked on which days, in order that all could plan ahead.

Caitlyn Collins, in her book *Making Motherhood Work*, presents a damning picture of US policies for working mothers. Focusing primarily on the situation of middle-class, working mothers, she concluded, "Countries like Sweden, Germany, and Italy have built rescue boats for the particular waters they [working mothers] trawl, some better than others. The US has largely chosen to forgo the rescue boats."[5] What are new parents to do when their baby has been up all night with a fever, they can't bring their baby to day care, they have no personal or sick time, and they will be fired if they don't show up to work? These types of squalls, and outright storms, are likely to swamp even the most steady ships. There are currently few supports in place to bolster up families in the United States: we have no rescue boats.

## All in a Day's Work: Better Jobs, Better Parents

Another important theme from our research is that while some low-wage jobs are monotonous, stressful, and unsatisfying, others are experienced by workers as empowering, enjoyable, and satisfying. For example, Brianna talked about the satisfaction of making a healthy lunch for the elderly client she served. "This seems like important work. In little ways I am making her life better, and that makes my life better. Jesus says, 'Do unto others,' and that is what I am doing." Vince, who worked in a food warehouse facility, also loved his job. He talked about the tight connection among his coworkers: "We are like a family.

They are all so excited about this baby and have been so supportive of me and Lisa [his wife]. They gave us a baby shower and everything." He also talked about his job as "fun." "I get to ride around in forklifts and organize the system. I like to be orderly. I am good at this." An important theme arising from this research is that parents' experiences, day in and day out, over weeks, months, and years, have a profound impact on them, on their well-being and health, and on their partners and children. So, how do we make work better?

*Reform low-income jobs to provide autonomy and dignity.* When I've presented the stories from this book at conferences, some colleagues have railed against these examples. "These are Band-Aids," they object. These approaches simply serve to "keep the low-wage worker happy and in their place." I take this criticism seriously. I hardly want this work to be interpreted as naive or as suggesting that employers should simply placate disgruntled workers, rather than provide workers with more substantive benefits. While it is true that wages remain too low and supportive policies too rare, this should not overshadow the importance of feeling valued, respected, and engaged on the job. We heard again and again from new parents how being treated with dignity and respect on the job translated to better parenting at home.

*Train supervisors to provide autonomy and support to workers.* Many of the examples provided in this book involve stressful, monotonous work, where workers felt disrespected and demoralized. These experiences often had less to do with the type of job than with rigid employer polices or unsupportive supervisors. As Gabbi described her office job, "I pretty much enter data all day. Now they time you on your start time and end time and check to see how much you did. You are not supposed to talk to your coworkers, only on set breaks. I can't even listen to music." She described the supervision as "heavy," since her supervisor had a desk in their office area. Gabbi felt badly for her supervisor: "She has a terrible job too. She has to walk around and discipline people who don't do their jobs fast enough. They don't pay us enough for this kind of treatment." Gabbi talked about going home and "flopping on the couch" at the end of the day, noting that "it is weird, but the boredom is exhausting."

Alana worked as a "facilities services assistant," or in her words, "I am a janitor in a hospital." She described walking around "on pins and needles because you are afraid of making a mistake" and felt her supervisor was overly vigilant in his use of a "point system" to penalize workers. Workers received points for a list of offenses, such as coming in late, leaving early, taking a sick day, and taking unscheduled breaks. Once a worker reached twelve points, they were fired. As Alana described, "They like to keep a paper trail on everything; they write you up if you're late, they write you up if you call out. I'm not comfortable with a paper trail that can make you lose your job." As she talked about her job, she gave a short laugh. "I could work at McDonalds and make the same pay." I asked Alana if companies ever offered ways for employees to "earn points" for a job well done, as opposed to always losing points. She laughed out loud, "Wouldn't that be nice." Not only nice, but, in my view, eminently doable!

It is not difficult to think of fairly simple, low-cost changes that could be made at these work sites to provide some autonomy and support to workers. Supervisors could meet with workers to solicit their input about how to improve work conditions and try out some pilot projects initiated by the workers. For example, one parent described how her supervisor at a paper plant had lunch with his employees once a week and often talked to them about how they could make their work site more efficient and productive. He also asked how he could make their jobs "more fun." Providing autonomy and support at work would, I believe, increase worker morale, retention, and attendance, but it also has the potential to improve workers' ability to parent at home and to enhance children's development.

The idea that having some control in your work life promotes job satisfaction is not a new idea. However, what is often overlooked, and what our research makes clear, is that low-wage factory jobs, food service jobs, and retail jobs can have many of the same characteristics as higher-income jobs. Low-wage workers can experience autonomy, control, and supportive relationships. As working parents told us, when supervisors include them in decision making, respect their ideas, give them some say in how they perform their work, acknowledge them as parents, and accommodate the unforeseen demands of parenting, workers feel better about their jobs. Implicit in this model, however, is that supervisors need to be empowered to create change, often a hard job for middle managers.

A simple way to start this process is to talk to workers themselves. Workers know what would make their jobs better, and many of their recommendations would cost little, even if they might require some flexibility and perhaps some creativity. Secondly, supervisors need to have the power and flexibility to modify work to suit workers better. This may require additional management training. In their work with high-tech IT industry, sociologists Erin Kelly and Phyllis Moen showed that increasing worker autonomy and flexibility through improved supervisor training resulted in happier and more satisfied workers. While low-wage work will not always be amenable to the same kinds of flexibility as higher-wage work—few low-wage jobs can be done from home, for instance—the more general lesson is that giving workers a voice in modifying their own work conditions will make work more family friendly.[6]

The idea behind much of what I have learned from this project is supported by Shelley Correll's research aimed at transforming organizations and reducing the negative effects of gender bias in the workplace.[7] She proposes a "small wins" model of change that focuses on researchers and managers working to produce concrete, implementable actions that produce visible results. In applying this step-by-step process to the challenges facing low-wage workers, I think it would be invaluable to add workers to this planning process, as well as in the evaluation of what works. As Correll argues, these "small, imperfect and incomplete" actions often lead to the larger organizational transformations that everyone is shooting for. I am not arguing that we give up on the large policy changes, such as paid leave; we need big change. But I am proposing that a "small wins" approach can provide the building blocks to greater change, and—the best part—it can begin tomorrow.

## Uncovering the Full Story: Implications for Researchers

My team and I have learned invaluable lessons along the way about conducting research that is true to the complexity of family life. Although it often seemed appealing to look past the messiness of family life that we witnessed during our interviews—to stick rigidly to the protocol, collect our questionnaires, and move on—had we done so, we would have missed out on tremendous insights into the unique issues faced by low-income workers.

For instance, I started this project with the idea that more objective data, such as hours or schedules, would be the easiest information to quantify. It seemed simple enough to ask participants about how many hours they worked and what their schedules were; however, this turned into an especially challenging task with a low-wage worker for a number of reasons. First, many of these occupations, such as service work and agricultural jobs, are subject to seasonal variations, leading to unstable and varied work hours. For example, in our sample, we found that over a year's time, more than one-third of our parents changed jobs, and another third added a second (or third) job or dropped a job. As poverty researchers Greg Duncan and Katherine Magnuson have demonstrated, 25 percent of people living in poverty one year have incomes above the poverty level the next year, because of movement into and out of jobs.[8] Moreover, many of the parents we talked to worked alternating shifts that varied over the course of a month. Parents would often pull out their calendar and share with us their typical schedules over the past two weeks or month. We had to completely restructure our interview materials to capture these complex and shifting work schedules. Family-work researchers need to be open to capturing the variability, instability, and unpredictability of parents' work and family lives, even when the data do not fit easily on forms and questionnaires.

In this study our "default" family was the nuclear family. Although we knew from trips into families' homes that many parents lived in far more complex family systems, and we made some attempts to capture this complexity, our efforts did not go nearly far enough. The nuclear family unit of mother, father, and child is on the decline and does not represent the experience of the typical American family, and our families proved that reality. Our measures and interviews fell far short in reflecting how these complex family systems operated. Although we asked many questions about social support and relationships with parents, siblings, extended kin, and friends, we only peripherally included them in the interview process, even when some of these individuals lived within the same home. Only in the case of our single mothers did we make a step in that direction. We had each single mother identify one person as a secondary caregiver—her own mother, her sister, her friend, her boyfriend, or the baby's biological father—and we interviewed that person as well. In retrospect, I believe the best way to have approached this topic would have been to ask parents who they consider their family and decide whom to interview based on their responses.

More than half of the families we interviewed included at least one other kin member, and many contained multiple family members. These family members often provided child care, social support, monetary support, and emotional support to our new parents. This was particularly true for ninety-six single mothers in our study, all but ten of whom had other family members living with them at one point during the first year. In addition, family structure is not necessarily stable. In our first project, involving coupled parents, the majority stayed stably coupled for the first year, and only seven had split up. Six years later, 126 out of 153 were still together. In contrast, in our second project, involving more diverse family structures, there was tremendous variability even across the first year. Of the ninety-six single mothers, seventy-one stayed single across the first year, while twenty-five became coupled over the year. Of the cohabiting mothers, fifty-eight remained cohabiting across the first year, while twenty-two split up with their partner. Among the thirty-one married couples, only one separated during the first year. Thus, in just the span of the first year, close to 25 percent of couples in our study changed their family structure, an event that often creates an added level of stress for parents and children. In theorizing and research involving families, academics need to keep in mind that family structure is a dynamic process rather than a static variable.

Although we fell short in capturing a complete picture of the busy and changing households of our families, a tremendous

amount was gained by giving mothers and fathers equal attention in every aspect of our project. Most importantly, our findings show that fathers, like mothers, are affected by their work
experiences, and that their work has implications for their
mental health, their parenting, and their children's development. The highly gendered research on work and family reflects
the societal view that parenting is primarily women's work, with
"help" from men. Despite the fact that this gendered division
of labor favors men and overloads women, our research often
reflects this bias as well. There is far more research on the relationship between mothers' employment and their children's
development than there is on the impact of fathers' employment. Our data suggest this is shortsighted and may uninten-
tionally reinforce the idea that fathers are less influential in their
children's lives than they are in fact.

As researchers, we must do better in capturing the full ex-
panse of families' work and family lives. Our tried-and-true
methods and statistics often move us to "control" for variability
as opposed to exploring it. Interdisciplinary endeavors that
challenge us to capture the complexity of work and family, with
insights and perspectives from psychologists, sociologists, and
economists, are needed to understand how macro-level factors
in the economy and policies shape micro-level processes linking work and families.

## Jobs and Babies: The First Time Around

The confluence of two critical life events shaped the experiences of the families that participated in our study—having a
child and returning to paid work after birth. Many young, first-
time parents have not even established themselves in secure,
full-time occupations yet are faced with the responsibilities of

establishing a financially secure household. Many of the working parents we talked to had minimal job experience and little familiarity with the norms and regulations attached to full-time employment. Thus, when they made a mistake like coming in late or failing to give enough notice for a personal day, it could lead to penalties and warnings that eventually resulted in being fired. Few had parents, caretakers, or role models who taught them about being on time for work, dressing appropriately, saving some earnings, or asking bosses in advance for time off for appointments. They had not been taught the "hidden agenda" of work. For young adults from middle- and upper-class families, with built-in safety nets of parents and kin, mistakes in one's first job can be chalked up to a lesson learned, where the only thing worse for wear is one's morale or pride. For the majority of young, low-income parents, however, making a mistake and losing one's job could easily lead them down the slippery slope of unemployment, homelessness, and poverty.

The lack of mentoring and modeling about how to "do work" was staggering. I witnessed many instances where if a parent overslept for work or could not find a babysitter, he or she decided not to go to work at all, rather than calling to talk to the boss. These parents had little experience in making requests of their bosses or negotiating a day off when their child was ill. This project was not an intervention—we did not set out to "fix" anything. It was clear to me, however, that had I been a friend, an aunt, or some type of mentor to many of these young parents, I might have been able to offer strategies to cope with work and supervisors. Perhaps a workplace mentor model, where more senior employees are assigned to support new workers, might be put into place. These mentors could show new workers the ropes, educate them about the informal culture of the job, and socialize them into the world of work. The fear in offering this kind of suggestion is that it focuses on personal changes the employee might make, rather than identifying structural changes that employers could make. However, policy changes and employer interventions can go hand in hand with greater employee support and socialization.

As policy makers consider solutions to better support working families in this country, they must not overlook the broader social climate that surrounds these initiatives. The twenty-first century has been an age of staggering economic and social inequality, a time when the wages for low-income workers have been stagnating or declining. This course of events is frustrating and discouraging for anyone who cares about living in a fair society, particularly because the social forces bringing about these outcomes often seem far removed from everyday life. As I have argued, big policy change is needed: higher wages, paid parental leaves, sick time. Yet our data also suggest that small-scale efforts to improve workplaces could significantly improve the lives of workers and their families, especially children. Large-scale policy change coupled with small-scale efforts in workplaces can, and should, occur at the same time. If our society is truly committed to giving the next generation of children in this country a healthy and equal start, an obvious place to look for change is the workplace. As we transform workplaces to be places where all workers can be engaged and productive, autonomous and respected, not only do we enhance the health and well-being of workers and build stronger and more productive organizations—we build a society where the next generation can flourish. We can start now!

# APPENDIXES

## Appendix A: Notes on Theory and Empirical Research

### *Theoretical Background*

Numerous theories have been proposed to explain how work conditions influence workers' own mental and physical health as well as the quality of their family relationships. Theoretical frameworks from a variety of disciplines, such as developmental psychology, sociology, social psychology, health psychology, economics, and labor studies, address the bidirectional processes linking work and family.[1] At an overarching level, however, sitting above particular theories that speculate about processes, an ecological perspective challenges us to consider how the mechanisms that connect work and family life may differ dramatically within social contexts, and ultimately hold different consequences for human development.

#### BRONFENBRENNER'S ECOLOGICAL PERSPECTIVE

Research has documented many ways that different social contexts, such as social class or race, can alter the ways that work and family intersect.[2] [3] For example, findings have shown that full-time work hours for mothers in middle-class households predict higher stress; however, full-time hours in single-mother households protect against stress, primarily because in the latter case mothers are sole providers and full-time work often raises them out of poverty.[4] This is an example of how connections between work and family may work in opposite ways within unique family contexts.

In another example, Susan Lambert and colleagues showed us how the notion of "schedule flexibility," presumably a good thing, actually held negative consequences for some low-wage workers.[5] In short, her data showed that when scheduling flexibility policies were instituted among low-wage, service workers, a policy where workers could submit ahead of time what shifts they could work and request some flexibility, those requesting flexibility were assigned *fewer* work hours. Basically, it was easier for supervisors to assign more hours to those workers who had no limits on their schedules than those who requested times that they could coordinate with child care. In this case, instituting "schedule flexibility" policies resulted in some low-wage workers, usually parents responsible for young children, losing valuable paid hours.

Another example from my own earlier work addresses how social context can differentially shape processes within families. We examined how socioeconomic status (SES) shaped the ways in which the division of paid and unpaid labor in families was related to married couples' relationship quality.[6] A great deal of research has documented the unfair and gendered division of household and child-care chores that disadvantages women, even when men and women work equal hours in paid work. Using data from the National Survey of Families and Households (NSFH), we defined four types of social class dyads: (1) both spouses were defined as working class based on each spouse's level of education and income, (2) both spouses were middle class, (3) husband was working class / wife was middle class, and (4) husband was middle class / wife was working class. The idea was that class plays out *within* families, between husbands and wives, not simply between families.

We found that for middle-class women who were married to either middle-class or working-class men, the more unfair the division of family labor, the more marital conflict was reported by both husbands and wives. Thus, for wives with higher levels of income and education, an unequal division of labor was a source of significant conflict. In contrast, for working-class women married to either middle- or working-class men, a more unequal division of labor (meaning wives performed more tasks than their husbands) was related to *less* marital conflict for both spouses. In this case, women with lower levels of income and education than their spouses did more tasks, but this inequality was not related to marital conflict. Why? Because working-class women saw their unequal load of housework as more "fair" than their more affluent counterparts saw it and, thus, were less likely to fight with their spouses about it.

These few examples point to the ways in which social contexts, like social class, can shape work-family processes in different ways. An ecological perspective considers how contexts outside of the developing child, such as parents' work, or class inequality, can ultimately shape child development.[7] How does parents' work seep into the family? What are the processes that bring work home? Do these processes differ in different social contexts? Two theories have been prominent in hypothesizing about how work shapes the lives of families: work socialization theory and work spillover theory.

## THE WORK SOCIALIZATION THEORY

A work socialization perspective holds that work conditions reinforce values and beliefs in workers. Workers are socialized to accept certain values and norms at work (e.g., being prompt, not questioning authority), and then they bring those values home with them. Kohn posits that work experiences are echoed in parenting styles, such that parents socialize certain behaviors in their children that are valued at work.[8] For example, fathers working under conditions of high supervision and limited autonomy are likely to use more controlling and punitive parenting styles in the home, which in turn, predicts more negative child outcomes. In an extension of Kohn's work, Stacy, Rogers, and Menaghan found that workers who experienced a sense of control at work were more likely to promote supportive and less controlling home environments for children.[9] By extension, those reporting less control at work exhibited more overreactive and controlling parenting behavior leading to more behavior problems (e.g., aggression, hyperactivity) in children.[10]

## WORK SPILLOVER THEORY

Another way that conditions of work have been theorized to affect parents and children is through both *positive and negative work-to-family spillover*, a phenomenon whereby work strains have a negative effect on family life while positive conditions of work bode well for family life.[11] Negative spillover may cause *role strain*, wherein mothers may feel that their roles as parents and workers are incompatible, leading to increased stress, poorer mental health outcomes, and difficulty keeping steady employment.[12][13] Specifically, a lack of supportive policies may predict more negative work-to-family spillover, which, in turn, predicts poorer mental health; conversely, supportive policies can decrease spillover and enhance mental health. Jang and colleagues[14] found that negative work-to-family spillover mediated the link between family-friendly policies and workers' stress, such that supportive policies reduced negative spillover, which, in turn, reduced stress. Similarly, Goodman and Crouter found that greater schedule flexibility led to reduced spillover, which, in turn, predicted fewer depressive symptoms among working parents.[15] Researchers have called for further studies to explore how negative spillover works as a mechanism linking work policies to mothers' and fathers' depression, especially during the vulnerable period of new parenthood.[16]

## Review of the Empirical Literature

Although a great deal of research has examined the relationship between maternal employment, primarily hours and schedules, and children's development,[17] less is known about how employees' experiences at work, such as autonomy, self-direction, and relationships with supervisors and coworkers, are related to children's developmental outcomes, such as problem behaviors or good social skills. There are a few examples. Roeters, Van der Lippe, and Kluwer found that parents who worked fewer hours and had more engaging jobs spent more time with their children, which, in turn, predicted higher-quality parent-child relations.[18] Walker, Updegraff, and Crouter found that, among Mexican-origin families, fathers' occupational self-direction was linked to less parent-adolescent conflict and, in turn, better adolescent adjustment.[19] These studies suggest that more autonomy at work translates into more proactive and supportive parenting behaviors at home. In contrast, parents who worked in controlling environments, with little autonomy, would be more likely to bring those behaviors home in the form of being more controlling and rigid. Turning to supervisor behavior, Gassman-Pines found supervisor criticism during the workday predicted more withdrawn parenting behavior at home. Thus, we have evidence that work conditions can affect parenting and children, but there are some gaps in our knowledge.[20]

First, one potential problem underlying much of the research linking parental work conditions to child development is the practice of assigning characteristics of occupations, as defined by the *Dictionary of Occupational Titles* (2003),[21] to workers' experiences of their jobs.[22] [23] Although this is a creative approach to linking work characteristics to workers' jobs in the absence of subjective reports, it assumes that all individuals working in a particular occupation experience the same levels of complexity and autonomy at work. Such an approach would code the majority of working-class jobs as low in autonomy, an assumption that research has shown to be unfounded. In short, jobs in a particular social class strata are not experienced in the same way by all workers.[24] From a policy perspective, it is important to understand what conditions of low-prestige jobs can be experienced as autonomous, as this knowledge could improve the development of effective interventions focused on enhancing job conditions for low-income, working parents.

A second shortcoming in the literature is that we know surprisingly little about how fathers' employment, whether hours or social conditions of work or both, is related to the development of their children. Sociologist Kathleen Gerson argues that the current culture of fatherhood calls for men to be not only workers but also involved fathers and equal partners.[25] Two studies from the Family Life Project found that greater paternal work stress was related to poorer-quality parenting with infants. In addition, when fathers worked more hours on a nonstandard shift, they were less likely to be sensitive and engaged parents.[26] [27] In contrast, Costigan, Cox, and Cauce found that fathers' job autonomy and coworker relations were unrelated to parenting quality with infants.[28] More research is needed to better understand the long-term implications of fathers' work, especially during the transition to fatherhood when child-care and involvement patterns are just being established, for children's later development.

Yet another challenge to our understanding of how parents' work affects children is our lack of attention to how children's developmental stage may make them more or less susceptible to the influences of parental work. To that end, recent research has begun to focus on the issue of timing, specifically examining the impact of parental employment during the first years of a child's life. The theoretical argument for how and why early parental employment, most often conceptualized as maternal employment, might affect child development stems from an extensive literature in developmental psychology that points to the quality of the early parent-child relationship in shaping children's socioemotional and cognitive development.[29] Parents provide a secure base for early infant development as well as providing support and scaffolding to enrich social relationships and cognitive development. Given the critical role of parents in early development, concerns that early maternal employment may impinge on mothers' time and ability to develop secure and nurturing relationships with their children spurred the focus on maternal employment in the first years of a child's life.

A number of studies provide support for the early life experience hypothesis. Costigan, Cox, and Cauce found that mothers' reports of more negative interpersonal relationships at work predicted decreases in positive parenting of their infant from nine to twelve months of age.[30] Looking at much longer time frames, Yetis-Bayraktar, Budig, and Tomaskovic-Devey found that mothers' concurrent occupational complexity, defined as autonomy and supervisory responsibilities, was positively related to their six-to-thirteen-year-old children's academic achievement.[31] In addition, mothers' occupational complexity in the first three years of the child's life was related to children's later positive academic outcomes in school, with enhanced advantages for boys' math abilities. Fathers' work conditions were not found to be related to parenting. Relatedly, Brooks-Gunn, Han, and Waldfogel found that early maternal employment in the first three months of a child's life predicted more externalizing behaviors at 4.5 years; however, maternal sensitivity and a positive home environment buffered this negative relationship.[32] A considerable research base provides evidence that early parental employment may be critical in setting the stage for later developmental outcomes in children, and that process is partly mediated through parenting styles.

In the current research, the question is whether the social ecological niche of being in a low-income family uniquely shapes the ways in which work-family processes play out. Lucas-Thompson, Goldberg, and Prause conducted a meta-analysis of sixty-nine studies to synthesize the research linking maternal employment during infancy and early childhood to children's developmental outcomes. They found that, with few exceptions, "early employment was not significantly associated with later achievement or internalizing/externalizing behaviors" in children.[33] Follow-up analyses revealed, however, that social class moderated these findings such that early employment had modest but beneficial effects on children's outcomes in low-income families, and slightly more negative effects in high-SES families.

When looking within samples of low-income families, a number of studies have found positive associations with maternal employment early in children's lives and positive child out-comes.[34] [35] [36] It has been hypothesized that the benefits of maternal employment in low-SES contexts, where jobs bring economic stability and financial resources, may outweigh the potentially negative effects of decreased maternal time with children. Coley and Lombardi found, in a low-income, working sample of African-American and Hispanic families, that children whose mothers were employed early had enhanced socioemotional functioning in comparison to their peers with nonemployed mothers.[37] Utilizing the same data, Lombardi and Coley found that mothers with high work quality (i.e., income and insurance) and job stability had children with higher reading and math skills and fewer emotional and behavioral problems than mothers with low-quality jobs.[38] These authors' conceptualization of work quality, focusing on wages and insurance, clearly moves research beyond the past emphasis on maternal work status or work hours; however, questions remain as to how workers' experiences of low-income jobs, such as perceptions of autonomy, urgency, coworker support, and supervisor relations, are related to parent quality and child well-being.

Over the past decade, a number of books have brought to life the challenges of those at the lower end of the class spectrum, including the working class, the working poor, the marginally employed, and the poor.[39] [40] [41] [42] Ethnographies and mixed-methods studies document how both the economy and economic and social policies have left low-income families isolated, entrenched, with no safety net when trouble hits, and, often, with little hope for the future. At the same time, they highlight the resilience that keeps them going. Our project builds on these stories but focuses the lens a bit more, examining how the economic challenges of working parents (all in low-income jobs) affect family life at a critical time: the birth of a child. How does parents' work, both in its structural aspects (i.e., hours, schedules, stability) and in day-to-day experiences of it (i.e., autonomy, urgency, relationships with coworkers and supervisors) shape the early health and well-being of children?

The study described in this book relied on components of an ecological perspective as well as work socialization and work spillover theories to develop hypotheses and test research questions. By and large, we found support for the idea that conditions of work do spill over to shape child development via parents. Specifically, work affected parents' mental health, which in turn shaped their parenting. Similarly, work had an effect on children via parenting. Work conditions that energized workers "spilled over" to more engaged and sensitive parenting.

The work socialization perspective was also supported in our findings. For example, we found that parents' experiences of self-direction and autonomy at work predicted parenting styles that reinforced autonomy in children by reducing harsh and intrusive parenting. Consistent with the work of many scholars,[43] [44] [45] our data suggest that values and skills from work, focused on self-direction and autonomy, are transmitted to children through less overreactive parenting styles and more engaged parent involvement. These finding reinforce the work of others that have documented that more self-directed and complex work was more important than work status alone in relation to the quality of parenting.[46] [47] [48] What is unique about our findings is that we found examples of self-direction and autonomy within the jobs of low-income workers. Our study highlights the fact that even workers in low-income jobs can experience autonomy, self-direction and occupational complexity at work that can make them better parents. We also found that fathers' work matters as much as mothers' for parenting, mental health, and child development. Finally, given the burgeoning research on child development highlighting the first year of life as a particularly sensitive period in infant development,[49] we show that work conditions during this time play a critical role in shaping employed parents' ability to be engaged and sensitive caretakers, ultimately influencing children's development.

## Publications from the Work and Family Transition Project (WFTP)

As noted in the opening chapter, over the years a number of empirical, quantitative studies have been published with the WFTP data. All the summaries presented in the previous chapters are based on these peer-reviewed papers, which are listed below.

### PEER-REVIEWED ARTICLES

Barry, A. B., Smith, J. Z., Deutsch, F. M., and Perry-Jenkins, M. (2011). "Fathers' Involvement in Child Care and Perceptions of Parenting Skill over the Transition to Parenthood." *Journal of Family Issues*, 32 (11), 1500–1521.

Claxton, A., and Perry-Jenkins, M. (2008). "You're No Fun Anymore: Leisure and Marital Quality across the Transition to Parenthood." *Journal of Marriage and Family*, 70 (1), 28–43.

Craft, A. L., Perry-Jenkins, M., and Newkirk, K. (2021). "The Implications of Early Marital Conflict for Children's Development." *Journal of Child and Family Studies*, 30, 292–310. doi:10.1007/s10826-020-01871-6.

Goldberg, A., and Perry-Jenkins, M. (2004). "The Division of Labor and Working-Class Women's Well-Being across the Transition to Parenthood." *Journal of Family Psychology*, 18, 225–36.

Goldberg, A., Smith, J., and Perry-Jenkins, M. (2012). "The Division of Labor in Lesbian, Gay and Heterosexual Newly Adoptive Couples." *Journal of Marriage and Family*, 74 (4), 812–28.

Goldberg, A. E., and Perry-Jenkins, M. (2007). "The Division of Labor and Perceptions of Parental Roles: Lesbian Couples across the Transition to Parenthood." *Journal of Social and Personal Relationships*, 24, 297–318.

Halpern, H. P., and Perry-Jenkins, M. (2016). "Parents' Gender Ideology and Gendered Behavior as Predictors of Children's Gender-Role Attitudes: A Longitudinal Exploration." *Sex Roles*, 74 (11–12), 527–42. doi:10.1007/s11199-015-0539-0.

Hayes, U. L., Balaban, S., Smith, J. Z., Perry-Jenkins, M., and Powers, S. I. (2010). "Role of Pelvic Sensory Signaling during Delivery in Postpartum Mental Health." *Journal of Reproductive and Infant Psychology*, 28 (3), 307–23.

Herman, R., Meghani, D. T., Craft, A., and Perry-Jenkins, M. (forthcoming). "New Mothers' Sensitive Parenting: Implications of Work and Well-Being." *Journal of Child and Family Studies.*

Herman, R., and Perry-Jenkins, M. (2020). "Low-Wage Work Conditions and Mother-Infant Interaction Quality across the Transition to Parenthood." *Journal of Child and Family Studies*, 29 (12), 3552–64.

Keeton Pierce, C., Perry-Jenkins, M., and Sayer, A. (2008). "Sense of Control and Psychological Well-Being during the Transition to Parenthood." *Journal of Family Psychology*, 22 (2), 212–21.

Meteyer, K. B., and Perry-Jenkins, M. (2009). "Dyadic Parenting and Children's Externalizing Symptoms." *Family Relations*, 58 (3), 289–302.

Meteyer, K. B., and Perry-Jenkins, M. (2010). "Division of Childcare among Working-Class, Dual-Earner Couples." *Fathering: A Journal of Theory, Research and Practice about Men as Fathers*, 8 (3), 379–403.

Newkirk, K., Perry-Jenkins, M., Hein, M., and Laws, H. (2020). "Workplace Polices and Perinatal Depressive Symptoms among Low-Income, Single and Partnered Mothers." *Family Relations: An Interdisciplinary Journal of Applied Family Studies.* https://doi-org.silk.library.umass.edu/10.1111/fare.12471.

Newkirk, K., Perry-Jenkins, M., and Sayer, A. G. (2017). "Division of Household and Childcare Labor and Relationship Conflict among Low-Income New Parents." *Sex Roles: A Journal of Research*, 5–6, 319. doi:10.1007/s11199-016-0604-3.

Perry-Jenkins, M., and Claxton, A. (2011). "The Transition to Parenthood and the Reasons 'Momma Ain't Happy.'" *Journal of Marriage and Family*, 73 (1), 23–28.

Perry-Jenkins, M., Goldberg, A. E., Pierce, C. P., and Sayer, A. G. (2007). "Shift Work, Role Overload and the Transition to Parenthood." *Journal of Marriage and Family*, 69 (1), 123–38.

Perry-Jenkins, M., Goldberg, A., Smith, J. Z., and Logan, J. (2011). "Working-Class Jobs and New Parents' Mental Health." *Journal of Marriage and Family*, 73 (5), 1117–32.

Perry-Jenkins, M., Herman, R. J., Halpern, H. P., and Newkirk, K. (2017). "From Discovery to Practice: Translating and Transforming Work-Family Research for the Health of Families." *Family Relations*, 4, 614. doi:10.1111/fare.12267.

Perry-Jenkins, M., Laws, H., Sayer, A., and Newkirk, K. (2019). "Parents' Work and Children's Development: A Longitudinal Investigation of Working-Class

Families." *Journal of Family Psychology*, 34 (3), 257–68. https://doi-org.silk.library .umass.edu/10.1037/fam0000580.

Perry-Jenkins, M., Newkirk, K., and Ghunney, A. (2013). "Family Work through Time and Space: An Ecological Perspective." *Journal of Family Theory and Review*, 5 (2), 105–23.

Perry-Jenkins, M., Smith, J. Z., Wadsworth, L. P., and Halpern, H. P. (2017). "Workplace Policies and Mental Health among Working-Class, New Parents." *Community, Work and Family*, 20 (2), 226–49. doi:10.1080/13668803.2016.1252721.

Yoon, Y., Newkirk, K., and Perry-Jenkins, M. (2015). "Family Dinnertime Routines, Parenting Stress and Children's Social Development." *Family Relations*, 64 (1), 93–107.

## CHAPTERS

Haley, H., Perry-Jenkins, M., and Armenia, A. (2001). "Workplace Policies and the Psychological Well-Being of First-Time Parents: The Case of Working-Class Families." In R. Hertz and N. Marshall (Eds.), *Work and Family: Today's Realities and Tomorrow's Visions*. Berkeley: University of California Press.

Perry-Jenkins, M. (2004). "The Time and Timing of Work: Unique Challenges Facing Low-Income Families." In A. Crouter and A. Booth (Eds.), *Work-Family Challenges for Low-Income Parents and Their Children*, 107–16. Mahwah, NJ: Lawrence Erlbaum Associates.

Perry-Jenkins, M. (2005). "Work in the Working Class: Challenges Facing Workers and Their Families." In S. M. Bianchi, L. M. Casper, and R. B. King (Eds.), *Work, Family, Health and Well-Being*, 453–72. Mahwah, NJ: Erlbaum.

Perry-Jenkins, M. (2009). "Making a Difference for Hourly Workers: Considering Work-Life Policies in Social Context." In A. Booth and A. C. Crouter (Eds.), *Work-Life Policies That Make a Real Difference for Individuals, Families and Organizations*, 219–27. Washington, DC: Urban Institute Press.

Perry-Jenkins, M. (2012). "The Challenges to and Consequences of 'Opting Out' for Low-Wage, New Mothers." In B. D. Jones (Ed.), *Women Who Opt Out: The Debate over Working Mothers and Work-Family Balance*. New York: New York University Press.

Perry-Jenkins, M. (2016). "Women, Men, Work and Family: Action in the Interactions." In S. M. McHale, V. King, J. Van Hook, A. Booth, S. M. McHale, V. King, and A. Booth (Eds.), *Gender and Couple Relationships*, 131–38. Cham, Switzerland: Springer International. doi:10.1007/978-3-319-21635-5_7.

Perry-Jenkins, M. (2018). "Dual-Earner Families in Social Context." In M. Bornstein (Ed.), *Sage Encyclopedia of Lifespan Human Development*, 2:671. Thousand Oaks, CA: Sage.

Perry-Jenkins, M., Bourne, H., and Meteyer, K. (2007). "Work-Family Challenges for Blue-Collar Families." In T. Juravich (Ed.), *The Future of Work in Massachusetts*, 185–204. Amherst: University of Massachusetts Press.

Perry-Jenkins, M., and Claxton, A. E. (2009). "Feminist Visions for Rethinking Work and Family Connections." In S. Lloyd, A. Few, and K. Allen (Eds.), *Handbook of Feminist Family Studies*, 121–34. Thousand Oaks, CA: Sage.

Perry-Jenkins, M., Claxton, A. E., Smith, J., and Manning, M. A. (2009). "To Work and to Love: Bidirectional Relationships between Job Conditions and Marriage." In D. R. Crane and E. J. Hill (Eds.), *Handbook of Families and Work: Interdisciplinary Perspectives*, 374–91. New York: University Press of America.

Perry-Jenkins, M., and MacDermid, S. (2012). "Work and Family through Time and Space: Revisiting Old Themes and Charting New Directions." In G. W. Peterson and K. R. Bush (Eds.), *The Handbook of Marriage and the Family*, 549–72. New York: Springer.

Perry-Jenkins, M., and MacDermid, S. (2013). "The State of Theory in Work and Family Research at the Turn of the Twenty-First Century." In M. Fine and F. Fincham (Eds.), *Handbook of Family Theories: A Content-Based Approach*, 381–97. New York: Routledge.

Perry-Jenkins, M., Pierce, C. P., and Goldberg, A. E. (2004). "Discourses on Diapers and Dirty Laundry: Family Communication about Child Care and Housework." In A. Vangelisti (Ed.), *Handbook of Family Communication*. Mahwah, NJ: Lawrence Erlbaum Associates.

Perry-Jenkins, M., and Schoppe-Sullivan, S. (2018). "The Transition to Parenthood in Sociocultural Context." In B. Fiese and K. Deater-Deckard (Eds.), *Handbook of Contemporary Family Psychology*. Washington, DC: APA Press.

Perry-Jenkins, M., and Turner, E. (2004). "Jobs, Marriage and Parenting: Working It Out in Dual-Earner Families." In M. Coleman and L. H. Ganong (Eds.), *Handbook of Contemporary Families: Considering the Past, Contemplating the Future*. Thousand Oaks, CA: Sage.

## PUBLICATIONS INFORMED BY THE WORK AND FAMILY TRANSITION PROJECT

Perry-Jenkins, M., and Gerstel, N. (2020). "Work and Family in the Second Decade of the 21st Century." *Journal of Marriage and Family*, 1, 420. https://doi-org.silk.library.umass.edu/10.1111/jomf.12636.

Perry-Jenkins, M., and Gillman, S. (2000). "Parental Job Experiences and Children's Well-Being: The Case of Working-Class Two- and Single-Parent Families." *Journal of Family and Economic Issues*, 21 (2), 123–47.

Perry-Jenkins, M., Repetti, R., and Crouter, A. C. (2000). "Work and Family: A Decade Review." *Journal of Marriage and the Family*, 62 (4), 981–98.

Perry-Jenkins, M., and Wadsworth, S. M. (2017). "Capturing Complexities in Work and Family Theory and Research." *Journal of Family Theory and Review*, 2, 253. doi:10.1111/jftr.12190.

Perry-Jenkins, M., and Wadsworth, S. M. (2017). "Work and Family Research and Theory: Review and Analysis from an Ecological Perspective." *Journal of Family Theory and Review*, 2, 219. doi:10.1111/jftr.12188.

Pietromonaco, P. R., and Perry-Jenkins, M. (2014). "Marriage in Whose America? What the Suffocation Model Misses." *Psychological Inquiry*, 25 (1), 108–13.

Swanberg, J. E., Nichols, H. M., and Perry-Jenkins, M. (2016). "Working on the Frontlines in U.S. Hospitals: Scheduling Challenges and Turnover Intent among Housekeepers and Dietary Service Workers." *Journal of Hospital Administration*, 4, 76–86.

# Appendix B: The Work and Family Transitions Project

## *Methods, Sample, Measures, and Procedure*

The Work and Family Transitions Project (WFTP) encompasses two distinct longitudinal studies that were funded by the National Institute of Mental Health in the late 1990s and into the first decade of the twenty-first century. The first study includes 153 married (20 percent long-term cohabiters), working-class couples followed across the first year of parenthood. The second, a continuation project, follows up this married sample five years later and adds on a new sample of 207 low-income families, comprising primarily single and cohabiting women, with a small subsample of married women. Parents in both studies were experiencing the transition to parenthood. The aim of the overall project, which began in 1998, was to understand how low-wage work conditions and workplace policies across the transition to parenthood had short- and long-term implications for parents and children. Specifically, we were interested in examining how the employment of both mothers and fathers, early in their infants' lives, predicted parents' mental health, the quality of parental relationships, and, ultimately, children's developmental outcomes. Importantly, we wanted to look past the simple question of whether or not both parents were employed; rather, we sought to examine specific conditions of parents' work, such as scheduling flexibility, income, shift work, autonomy, time stress, and supervisor and coworker support as key factors influencing workers and their families. We focused exclusively on working-class and working-poor employees because much less is known about the unique challenges facing families with few economic and social supports than about their more often studied middle-class counterparts.

The first project, the Work and Family Transitions Project (WFTP) Study 1, was funded through a First Independent Research Support and Transitions (FIRST, NIH R29) award from the National Institute of Mental Health. Between 1998 and 2003 with a follow-up five years later, we interviewed 153 coupled families (78 percent White, 12 percent African American, 8 percent Latino, 2 percent Multiracial). Parents were recruited from prenatal classes, Women, Infants and Children (WIC) programs offices, and OB/GYN clinics in and around Springfield, Massachusetts. We had a number of criteria for participation. All parents had to be expecting their first child, be married or cohabiting for two years prior to pregnancy, be working full-time and planning on returning to full-time work, and have no higher than an associate's degree. All the couples who participated were either married (80 percent) or cohabiting, and all were expecting their first child. All parents were employed in low-wage occupations, the most typical being food service workers, truck drivers, certified nursing assistants, and factory workers. The average family income for this sample was $39,870.

Mothers and fathers were interviewed five separate times across the first year of parenthood. They were interviewed at the following time points: (1) during the couple's third trimester of pregnancy, (2) approximately one month after the baby's birth but before the mother had returned to full-time employment, (3) one month after the mother returned to full-time employment (sixteen weeks postpartum, on average), (4) six months postpartum, and (5) one year after the baby was born. At phases 1, 2, 3, and 5, interviews were conducted separately with both partners in their homes and were between two and three hours long; for phase 4 a packet of questionnaires was mailed to respondents. Detailed data were collected on parents' mental health, work conditions, relationship quality, social support, and parenting experiences (see list of measures below). Interviews included structured survey instruments as well as open-ended, qualitative components. Original interviews were repeated in a sixth phase of the study as the target child was entering the first grade. In addition, interactions between (a) couples and (b) parents and children were videotaped during home visits, and teachers completed assessments of children's academic and social outcomes in the school setting.

Between 2004 and 2009, we conducted a replication of Study 1, again funded by NIMH (MH 56477 R01), but with a more diverse sample in terms of family structure and race and ethnicity. The sample in Study 2 included 207 expectant mothers (forty-seven African American, seventy-five Latino, seventy-four White, and ten Multiracial families, and one Asian family). Ninety-six were single mothers, eighty were cohabiting, and thirty-one were married. All mothers were employed in low-income jobs. Mothers worked an average of thirty-four hours per

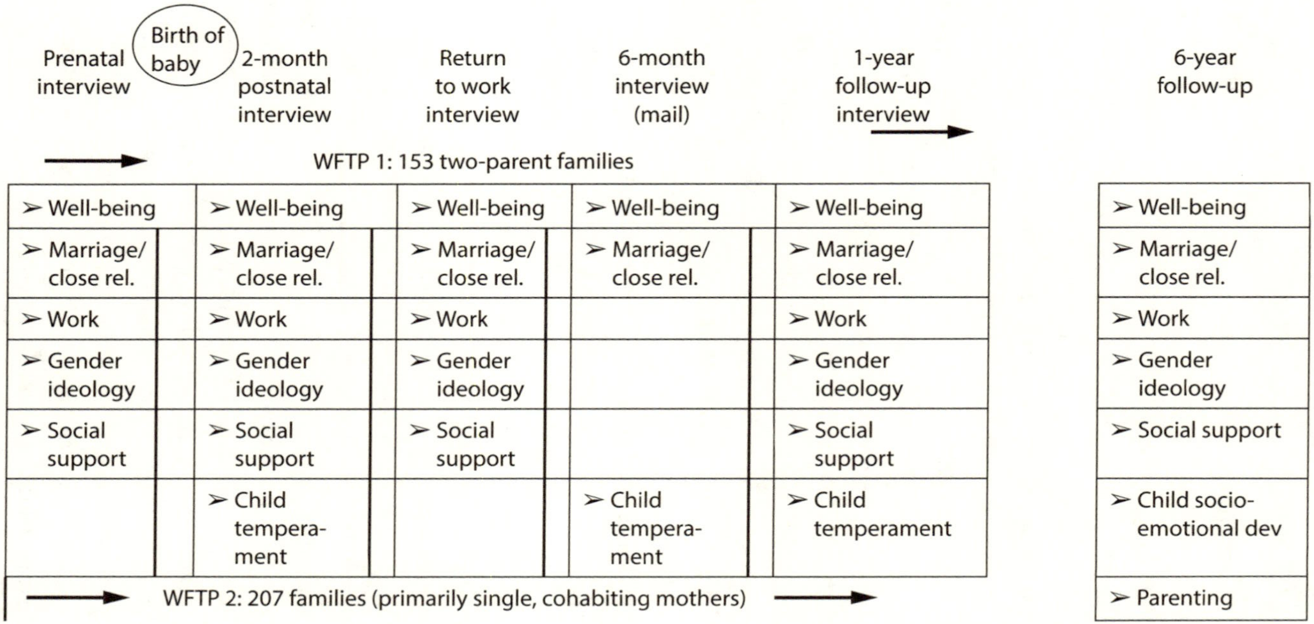

| Prenatal interview | Birth of baby → 2-month postnatal interview | Return to work interview | 6-month interview (mail) | 1-year follow-up interview | 6-year follow-up |
|---|---|---|---|---|---|
| ⋋ Well-being | ⋋ Well-being | ⋋ Well-being | ⋋ Well-being | ⋋ Well-being | ⋋ Well-being |
| ⋋ Marriage/close rel. | ⋋ Marriage/close rel. | ⋋ Marriage/close rel. | ⋋ Marriage/close rel. | ⋋ Marriage/close rel. | ⋋ Marriage/close rel. |
| ⋋ Work | ⋋ Work | ⋋ Work | | ⋋ Work | ⋋ Work |
| ⋋ Gender ideology | ⋋ Gender ideology | ⋋ Gender ideology | | ⋋ Gender ideology | ⋋ Gender ideology |
| ⋋ Social support | ⋋ Social support | ⋋ Social support | | ⋋ Social support | ⋋ Social support |
| | ⋋ Child temperament | | ⋋ Child temperament | ⋋ Child temperament | ⋋ Child socio-emotional dev |
| | | | | | ⋋ Parenting |

WFTP 1: 153 two-parent families

WFTP 2: 207 families (primarily single, cohabiting mothers)

FIGURE 12. Work and Family Transitions Project (WFTP) timeline used for data collection and key constructs assessed in the interviews.

WFTP Sample 1

| | Fathers (n = 153) | Mothers (n = 153) |
|---|---|---|
| Age | 27.2 (4.9) | 25.6 (3.8) |
| Education | HS/GED or less 23%<br>Tech training 63%<br>Assoc degree 14% | HS or less 34%<br>Tech training 54%<br>Assoc degree 12% |
| Income | $29,500 | $24,400 |
| Work hours | 47.2 | 40.0 |
| Yrs married/cohabiting | 3.4 | |

WFTP Sample 2

| | Single mothers (N = 89) | Cohabiting mothers (N = 85) | Married mothers (N = 33) |
|---|---|---|---|
| Age | 24.4 | 24.8 | 29.7 |
| Education | <H.S 16%<br>HS/GED 58%<br>Tech/Voc 26%<br>College 0% | <H.S 6%<br>HS/GED 65%<br>Tech/Voc 29%<br>College 0% | <H.S 4%<br>HS/GED 23%<br>Tech/Voc 73%<br>College 0% |
| Household income | $20,387 | $37,833 | $49,658 |
| Mothers' income | $20,387 | $19,291 | $26,644 |
| Work hours | 35.0 | 34.0 | 38.2 |

FIGURE 13. Descriptive data on the two samples.

week but ranged from ten to fifty-eight hours, and fathers worked a mean of forty-nine hours, with a range of thirty to seventy-one hours. The same data collection procedures were replicated in the second study. In addition, both mothers and fathers (when present) participated in parent-infant interactions when babies were three months and twelve months old, and these interactions were videotaped and coded for parenting sensitivity. Replicating the initial study with a more diverse sample allowed us to explore how race, ethnicity, and family structure provide unique contexts for the experiences of low-income employed new parents across the transition to parenthood.

The following list outlines the constructs we were interested in examining in the study and the measures used to assess them.

### Work and Family Transitions Project Measures

*Demographics*
- Family Information (size, structure)
- Employment Information (income, occupation, schedules, leave)
- Family Planning Questionnaire (was birth planned)
- Health Information (mental health, illnesses, pregnancy and birth health)

*Work*
- Benefits and Policies[50]
- Job Autonomy and Urgency[51]
- Supervisor Flexibility[52]
- Supervisor and Coworker Support[53]
- About Your Company[54]
- Work Preferences
- Open-Ended Work

*Family Roles*
- ▸ Provider Role Questionnaire[55]

*Gender Ideology*
- ▸ Attitudes toward Women Scale[56]
- ▸ Gender Ideology (Brogan and Kutner, 1976)[57]

*Well-Being*
- ▸ My Personality[58]
- ▸ Depression (Center for Epidemiological Studies)[59]
- ▸ Anxiety (Spielberger's State Anxiety Scale)[60]
- ▸ Role Overload[61]
- ▸ Self-Esteem[62]
- ▸ Sense of Control[63]
- ▸ Edinburgh Postnatal Depression Scale[64]
- ▸ Coping Scale[65]
- ▸ Open-Ended Well-Being

*Close Relationships*
- ▸ Personal Relationships Scale[66]
- ▸ Conflict Resolution Inventory[67]
- ▸ Leisure—Alone or with Others / with Partner (one form now)
- ▸ Quality of Relationships Inventory[68]—Partner
- ▸ Quality of Relationships Inventory—Secondary Caregiver
- ▸ Open-Ended Relationships Question—Partner
- ▸ Open-Ended Relationships Question—Secondary Caregiver

*Child Care*
- ▸ Beliefs about Child Care
- ▸ Involvement with Social Services
- ▸ Child-Care Plan

*Division of Labor*
- ▸ Who Does What / Household Chores[69]

- ► Division of Child-Care Tasks[70]
- ► Perceived Skill at Child Care[71]

*Social Support*

- ► Perceived Social Support—Family[72]
- ► Perceived Social Support—Friends[73]
- ► Religious Support / Religiosity[74]

*Race and Ethnicity*

- ► Racism on the Job[75]
- ► The Multigroup Ethnic Identity Measure (MEIM)[76]

*Family Beliefs and Rituals*

- ► Family Rituals[77]
- ► Upbringing and Parenting Questionnaire (open-ended version developed for the study)

*Parenting*

- ► Parent Involvement[78]
- ► Parent Overreactivity[79]
- ► Parenting Stress[80]

*Child Temperament and Behavior*

- ► The Infant Behavior Questionnaire—Short-Form Developmental Outcomes
- ► Behavioral Assessment System for Children Parent Rating Scales (BASC PRS)
- ► Behavioral Assessment System for Children Teacher Rating Scales (BASC RTS)
  - ▷ Assessments: hyperactivity, aggression, conduct problems, anxiety, depression, somatization, social skills, and leadership

*Parenting (self-report)*

- ► Parent Overreactivity / The Parenting Scale[81]
- ► Parenting Involvement / Alabama Parenting Questionnaire[82]

*Parent-Child Interactions*

▸ Parent-Infant Interactions

▷ The present study utilized a modified version[83] of the coding system used by the National Institute of Child Health and Human Development (NICHD) Study of Early Child Care.[84]

▷ Three domains of interaction quality were assessed: (1) responsiveness, (2) detachment, and (3) stimulation of development. These three dimensions of maternal caregiving quality were coded in one-minute intervals on a scale from 1 to 5, indicating the degree to which the behavior characterized the interaction. Each ten-minute free-play mother/father-child interaction was double-coded by two independent raters.

▸ Parents and Six-Year-Old Interactions

▷ A structured parent-child observation was conducted with each parent and the target child (mothers and fathers separately). Parent-child interactions were videotaped during two ten-minute interaction sequences. In the first ten-minute task (playtime), parent and child were given a set of toys to play with as they like. During the second ten-minute task (cleanup), parents were instructed to supervise their children putting the toys back in their containers. The goal of this procedure is to assess both positive and negative parental strategies as well as to assess child behavior.

▷ Coders reviewed the videotaped interactions and assigned global ratings on a scale from 1 to 7 for each parent on dimensions of *warmth, overreactivity,* and *laxness,* and each child on dimensions of *hyperactivity* and *hostile/defiant behavior.* Rating Scales from First Grade Parent-Child Interaction, Qualitative Rating Scales from the NICHD Study of Early Child Care were used to code child *agency* and *affection toward parent,* and two dyadic ratings of *goal-directed partnership* and *affective mutuality / felt security.*

## Qualitative Component of the Study

I want to be fully transparent that this study was originally conceptualized and funded as a quantitative project. As I described in chapter 2, we added in open-ended questions soon after we started collecting data, when we realized we were missing out on the thoughts and experiences parents often shared with us as they completed questionnaires. To that end, we added open-ended questions at the end of survey instruments to gain a better understanding of parents' thoughts and reflections. Thus, for example, after filling out a questionnaire about supervisor support or flexibility, we recorded parents' answers to open-ended prompts. We asked parents: Can you give me an example of when your supervisor was supportive or flexible? Can you give me an example of when you supervisor was unsupportive or inflexible. The goal was to get specific examples of what flexibility (or lack thereof) looked like for parents. We then used thematic analysis to code these open-ended responses based on an approach outlined by Braun and Clarke.[85]

I and my students were primary coders. First, I independently read through transcripts related to particular topics (e.g., workplace policies, parenting, supervisor support) to start understanding the data and developing preliminary themes. Using the supervisor support responses as an example, I generated initial codes such as "supportive," "negative," or "neutral" assessments. Within each broad theme I coded examples such as "gives me time when needed" or "was flexible with my parental leave." These codes then became the basis for "themes" such as "support with day-to-day schedule challenges" or "support after childbirth." At this point the second coder examined transcripts as a way to evaluate the emerging coding scheme and themes. We then organized the data in terms of the major themes that were prevalent across the sample of mothers and fathers for each topic discussed in the book (e.g., workplace policies, supervisor support, job autonomy). Quotations and examples from these final themes were used to provide the examples and stories that enrich the quantitative findings.

It should be noted that the quality of our qualitative data varied based on parents' engagement level, where some were very engaged and talkative and others had little to say beyond filling out the questionnaire.

I also used the qualitative data to develop the representative stories used at the beginning and ends of chapters. One advantage of having longitudinal data is that it allows for describing how work-family processes play out over time; the aim of the illustrative stories I tell in each chapter is to highlight change over time in work-family processes and to illustrate the unpredictable twists and turns that can occur for new parents. These stories were developed by examining both the quantitative and the qualitative data simultaneously to describe patterns and processes of family life across the course of new parenthood and beyond. In sum, I believe this use of mixed-methods, quantitative data to track change and variability in mental health or work conditions, for example, coupled with parents' explanations, feelings, and stories about their experiences allowed me to describe not only trends, means, and variability over time, but the personal joys and angst of new parents coping with jobs, relationships, babies, and the curve balls of life.

# NOTES

## Preface

1. The names of the people I talk about throughout this book have been changed.

## Chapter 1. "They Sure Don't Make It Easy for Parents": Low-Income, Working Parents and Their Children

1. This study was not an intervention, and I did not intend to shape the experiences of the young parents. Yet, as is true with most community-based projects, the mere process of sharing reflections, attitudes, and stories can influence the lives of participants.

2. Staff, J., and Mortimer, J. (2012), "Explaining the Motherhood Wage Penalty during the Early Occupational Career," *Demography*, 1, 1.

3. Budig, M. J., Misra, J., and Boeckmann, I. (2015), "Work-Family Policy Trade-Offs for Mothers? Unpacking the Cross-National Variation in Motherhood Earnings Penalties," *Work and Occupations*, 43 (2), 119–77.

4. "The Mommy Track," *Atlantic* (serial online), 2007:32, available from Literature Resource Center, Ipswich, MA, accessed June 5, 2018, https://www.theatlantic.com/business/archive/2014/02/the-mommy-track-myth/283557/.

5. BLS Reports, 2017, accessed October 30, 2021, https://www.bls.gov/opub/reports/minimum-wage/2016/home.htm.

6. Jou, J., Kozhimannil, K. B., Abraham, J. M., Blewett, L. A., and McGovern, P. M. (2018), "Paid Maternity Leave in the United States: Associations with Maternal and Infant Health," *Maternal and Child Health Journal*, 22 (2), 216–25, doi:10.1007/s10995-017-2393-x.

7. National Scientific Council on the Developing Child (2004), *Children's Emotional Development Is Built into the Architecture of Their Brains: Working Paper No. 2*, October 30, 2021, https://developingchild.harvard.edu/science/key-concepts/brain-architecture/.

8. "INBRIEF Series: The Science of Early Childhood Development," accessed October 30, 2021, https://46y5eh11fhgw3ve3ytpwxt9r-wpengine.netdna-ssl.com/wp-content/uploads/2007/03/InBrief-The-Science-of-Early-Childhood-Development2.pdf, 2.

## Chapter 2. "The Invisible Americans": The Work and Family Transitions Project

1. Kohn, M. (1977), *Class and Conformity: A Study in Values*, Homewood, IL: Dorsey.

2. Rubin, L. B. (1994), *Families on the Fault Line: America's Working Class Speaks about the Family, the Economy, Race, and Ethnicity*, New York: HarperCollins.

3. Kohn (1977), 48.

4. Rubin (1994).

5. Rubin (1994), 28.

6. See esp. Gilbert, D. (2015), *The American Class Structure in an Age of Growing Inequality*, Thousand Oaks, CA: Sage.

7. Catanzarite, L. (2003), *Wage Penalties in Brown-Collar Occupations*, Los Angeles: UCLA Chicano Studies Research Center, 2003.

8. Rose, S. J. (2016), Urban Institute, accessed October 31, 2021, https://www.urban.org/sites/default/files/publication/81581/2000819-The-Growing-Size-and-Incomes-of-the-Upper-Middle-Class.pdf.

9. Guzman, G. G. (2020), American Community Survey Briefs, accessed October 31, 2021, https://www.census.gov/content/dam/Census/library/publications/2020/acs/acsbr20-03.pdf.

10. Guzman, G. G. (2017), American Community Survey Briefs, accessed October 31, 2021, https://census.gov/content/dam/Census/library/publications/2017/acs/acsbr16-02.pdf.

11. Lambert, S. J., Haley-Lock, A., and Henly, J. R. (2012), "Schedule Flexibility in Hourly Jobs: Unanticipated Consequences and Promising Directions," *Community, Work and Family*, 15 (3), 293–315.

12. Komarovsky, M. (1967), *Blue-Collar Marriage*, New York: Vintage Books.

13. Rubin, L. B. (1976), *Worlds of Pain*, New York: Basic Books.

14. Rubin (1994), 28.

15. Levine, J. A. (2013), *Ain't No Trust: How Bosses, Boyfriends, and Bureaucrats Fail Low-Income Mothers and Why It Matters*, Berkeley: University of California Press.

16. Halpern-Meekin, S., Edin, K., Tach, L., and Sykes, J. (2015), *It's Not Like I'm Poor: How Working Families Make Ends Meet in a Post-Welfare World*, Oakland: University of California Press, retrieved January 20, 2020, www.jstor.org/stable/10.1525/j.ctt9qh29f.

17. Auyero, J., and Wacquant, L.J.D. (2015), *Invisible in Austin: Life and Labor in an American City*, Austin: University of Texas Press.

18. Crouter, A. C. and Booth, A. (2004), *Work-Family Challenges for Low-Income Parents and Their Children*, Mahwah, NJ: Lawrence Erlbaum Associates.

19. Seefeldt, K. S. (2016), *Abandoned Families: Social Isolation in the Twenty-First Century*, New York: Russell Sage Foundation.

20. Pugh, A. J. (2015), *The Tumbleweed Society: Working and Caring in an Age of Insecurity*, New York: Oxford University Press.

21. Edin, K. J., and Shaefer, H. L. (2015), *$2.00 a Day: Living on Almost Nothing in America*, Boston: Houghton Mifflin Harcourt.

22. Dyer, E. D. (1963), "Parenthood as Crisis: A Re-study," *Marriage and Family Living* 25:196–201.

23. Hobbs, D. F., Jr. (1965), "Parenthood as Crisis: A Third Study," *Journal of Marriage and the Family* 27:367–72.

24. Belsky, J., and Kelly, J. (1994), *The Transition to Parenthood*, New York: Delacorte.

25. Perry-Jenkins, M., and Schoppe-Sullivan, S. J. (2018), "The Transition to Parenthood in Sociocultural Context," in B. Fiese and K. Deater-Deckard (Eds.), *Handbook of Contemporary Family Psychology*, 463–82, Washington, DC: APA Press.

26. Gassman-Pines, A. (2011), "Associations of Low-Income Working Mothers' Daily Interactions with Supervisors and Mother-Child Interactions," *Journal of Marriage and Family*, 73 (1), 67–76.

27. Goodman, W. B., Crouter, A. C., Lanza, S. T., Cox, M. J., and Vernon-Feagans, L. (2011), "Paternal Work Stress and Latent Profiles of Father-Infant Parenting Quality," *Journal of Marriage and Family*, 73 (3), 588–604.

28. Gassman-Pines, A. (2015), "Effects of Mexican Immigrant Parents' Daily Workplace Discrimination on Child Behavior and Family Functioning," *Child Development*, 86 (4), 1175–90, https://doi-org.silk.library.umass.edu/10.1111/cdev.12378.

29. Foster, P. N., Santaniello, S. M., Calcina, J., Barbee, D., Fowlkes, K. (2006), Pioneer Valley Planning Commission, https://www.springfield-ma.gov/planning/fileadmin/Planning_files/Springfield_Market_Study_2006.pdf.

30. For more detail on methods, sample, and research challenges, see appendix B.

## Chapter 3. "A Little Can Go a Long Way": Workplace Policies and Parents' Well-Being

1. Bartel, A. P., Soohyun, K., Nam, J., Rossin-Slater, M., Ruhm, C., and Waldfogel, J. (2019), "Racial and Ethnic Disparities in Access to and Use of Paid Family and Medical Leave: Evidence from Four Nationally Representative Datasets," *Monthly Labor Review*, US Bureau of Labor Statistics, January, https://doi.org/10.21916/mlr.2019.2.

2. Moses-Kolko, E., and Roth, E. K. (2004), Antepartum and Postpartum Depression: Healthy Mom, Healthy Baby, *Journal of the American Medical Women's Association*, 59, 181–91.

3. Letourneau, N. L., Dennis, C., Cosic, N., and Linder, J. (2017), "The Effect of Perinatal Depression Treatment for Mothers on Parenting and Child Development: A Systematic Review," *Depression and Anxiety*, 34 (10), 928–66, doi:10.1002/da.22687.

4. Field, T. M. (2002), "Prenatal Effects of Maternal Depression," in S. H. Goodman, I. H. Gotlib, and S. H. Goodman (Eds.), *Children of Depressed Parents: Mechanisms of Risk and Implications for Treatment*, 59–88, Washington, DC: American Psychological Association, doi:10.1037/10449–003.

5. Center on the Developing Child at Harvard University (2009), *Maternal Depression Can Undermine the Development of Young Children: Working Paper No. 8*, accessed October 31, 2021, http://developingchild.harvard.edu/wp-content/uploads/2009/05/Maternal-Depression-Can-Undermine-Development.pdf.

6. Habib, C. (2012), Paternal Perinatal Depression: An Overview and Suggestions towards an Intervention Model, *Journal of Family Studies*, 18 (1), 4–16, doi:10.5172/jfs.2012.18.1.4.

7. US Department of Labor, accessed October 21, 2021, https://www.dol.gov/general/topic/benefits-leave/fmla.

8. Council of Economic Advisors, June 2014, Obama White House, accessed October 31, 2021, https://obamawhitehouse.archives.gov/sites/default/files/docs/leave_report_final.pdf.

9. Vogtman, J., and Schulman, K., 2016, National Women's Law Center, accessed October 31, 2021, https://nwlc.org/resources/set-up-to-fail-when-low-wage-work-jeopardizes-parents-and-childrens-success/, 1.

10. Adema, W., Clarke, C., and Thevenon, O., 2016, Social Policy Division, Organisation for Economic Co-operation and Development, accessed October 31, 2021, https://www.oecd.org/els/family/Backgrounder-fathers-use-of-leave.pdf.

11. Perry-Jenkins, M., Smith, J. Z., Wadsworth, L. P., and Halpern, H. P. (2017), Workplace Policies and Mental Health among Working-Class, New Parents, *Community, Work and Family*, 20 (2), 226–49, doi:10.1080/13668803.2016.1252721.

12. Tomfohr, L. M., Buliga, E., Letourneau, N. L., Campbell, T. S., and Giesbrecht, G. F. (2015), Trajectories of Sleep Quality and Associations with Mood during the Perinatal Period, *Sleep: Journal of Sleep and Sleep Disorders Research*, 38 (8), 1237–45, doi:10.5665/sleep.4900.

13. Dørheim, S. K., Bondevik, G. T., Eberhard-Gran, M., and Bjorvatn, B. (2009), Sleep and Depression in Postpartum Women: A Population-Based Study, *Sleep: Journal of Sleep and Sleep Disorders Research*, 32 (7), 847–55, doi:10.1093/sleep/32.7.847.

14. US Department of Labor, Wage and Hour Division, 2010, accessed October 31, 2021, https://www.dol.gov/whd/nursingmothers/.

15. Office on Women's Health, Department of Health and Human Services, 2014, accessed October 31, 2021, https://owh-wh-d9-dev.s3.amazonaws.com/s3fs-public/documents/fact-sheet-breastfeeding.pdf.

16. Center for Disease Control and Prevention, https://www.cdc.gov/mmwr/preview/mmwrhtml/mm6205a1.htm.

17. Center for Disease Control and Prevention, Progress Increasing Breastfeeding and Reducing Racial/Ethnic Differences—United States 2000–2008, 2013, accessed October 31, 2021, https://www.cdc.gov/prams/pdf/snapshot-report/breast-feeding.pdf.

18. Commonwealth of Massachusetts, Massachusetts Law about Employment Leave, 2019, accessed October 31, 2021, https://www.mass.gov/info-details/massachusetts-law-about-employment-leave#small-necessities-leave.

19. Economic Policy Institute, "The Cost of Child Care in Massachusetts," 2020, accessed October 31, 2021, https://www.epi.org/child-care-costs-in-the-united-states/#/MA.

20. Perry-Jenkins, M., Goldberg, A. E., Pierce, C. P., and Sayer, A. G. (2007), "Shift Work, Role Overload and the Transition to Parenthood," *Journal of Marriage and Family*, 69 (1), 123–38.

## Chapter 4. "They Treat Me Right, Then I Do Right by Them": Experiences in Low-Income Jobs and Mental Health

1. Office of the Press Secretary, White House Archives, 2014, "The Impact of Raising the Minimum Wage on Women and the Importance of Ensuring a Robust Tipped Minimum Wage," accessed October 31, 2021, https://obamawhitehouse.archives.gov/the-press-office/2014/03/26/new-white-house-report-impact-raising-minimum-wage-women-and-importance-.

2. Acs, G., Urban Institute, "Low-Income Workers and Their Employers," 2007, accessed October 31, 2021, https://www.urban.org/research/publication/low-income-workers-and-their-employers.

3. Haley-Lock, A., and Shah, M. F. (2007), "Protecting Vulnerable Workers: How Public Policy and Private Employers Shape the Contemporary Low-Wage Work Experience," *Families in Society*, 88 (3), 485–95, doi:10.1606/1044–3894.3659.

4. Yawen, C., Ichiro, K., Eugenie H. C., Joel, S., and Graham, C. (2000), "Association between Psychosocial Work Characteristics and Health Functioning in American Women: Prospective Study," *BMJ: British Medical Journal*, 7247, 1432.

5. Perry-Jenkins, M., Smith, J. Z., Goldberg, A. E., and Logan, J. (2011), "Working-Class Jobs and New Parents' Mental Health," *Journal of Marriage and Family*, 73 (5), 1117–32.

6. Hammer, L. B., Kossek, E. E., Anger, W. K., Bodner, T., and Zimmerman, K. L. (2011), "Clarifying Work-Family Intervention Processes: The Roles of Work-Family Conflict and Family-Supportive Supervisor Behaviors," *Journal of Applied Psychology*, 96 (1), 134, doi:10.1037/a0020927.

7. Roehling, P. V., Jarvis, L. H., and Swope, H. E. (2005), "Variations in Negative Work-Family Spillover among White, Black, and Hispanic American Men and Women: Does Ethnicity Matter?," *Journal of Family Issues*, 26 (6), 840–65, doi:10.1177/0192513X05277552.

8. Vazquez, C. I., and Clauss-Ehlers, C. S. (2005), "Group Psychotherapy with Latinas: A Cross-Cultural and Interactional Approach," *NYS Psychologist*, 17 (3), 10–13.

9. Bridges, J. S., and Etaugh, C. (1996), "Black and White College Women's Maternal Employment Outcome Expectations and Their Desired Timing of Maternal Employment," *Sex Roles*, 35 (9–10), 543–62, doi:10.1007/BF01548252.

10. Berger, L., Brooks-Gunn, J., Paxson, C., and Waldfogel, J. (2008), "First-Year Maternal Employment and Child Outcomes: Differences across Racial and Ethnic Groups," *Children and Youth Services Review*, 30 (4), 365–87, doi:10.1016/j.childyouth.2007.10.010.

11. Perry-Jenkins, M., and Gerstel, N. (2020), "Work and Family Issues in the Second Decade of the 21st Century," *Journal of Marriage and Family*, 1, 420, https://doi-org.silk.library.umass.edu/10.1111/jomf.12636.

12. Bureau of Labor Statistics, Office of Occupational Statistics and Employment Projections, "Occupations with the Most Job Growth," 2020, accessed October 31, 2021, https://www.bls.gov/emp/tables/occupations-most-job-growth.htm.

13. Brooks, G. (2007), "The Living Wage Movement: Potential Implications for the Working-Poor Families in Society," *Journal of Contemporary Social Services*, 88 (3), 438.

14. Kelly, E. L., Moen, P., Oakes, J. M., Fan, W., Okechukwu, C., Davis, K. D., Hammer, L. B., and Casper, L. M. (2014), "Changing Work and Work-Family Conflict: Evidence from the Work, Family, and Health Network," *American Sociological Review*, 79 (3), 485–516.

15. Linzer, M., Poplau, S., Grossman, E., Varkey, A., Yale, S., Williams, E., and Barbouche, M. (2015), "A Cluster Randomized Trial of Interventions to Improve Work Conditions and Clinician Burnout in Primary Care: Results from the Healthy Work Place (HWP) Study," *JGIM: Journal of General Internal Medicine*, 30 (8), 1105–11, doi:10.1007/s11606-015-3235-4.

16. Lambert, S. J., Haley-Lock, A., and Henly, J. R. (2012), "Schedule Flexibility in Hourly Jobs: Unanticipated Consequences and Promising Directions," *Community, Work and Family*, 15 (3), 293–315.

17. Hammer et al. (2011).

## Chapter 5. "This Parenting Thing Is Harder Than It Looks": Low-Income Work and Parenting

1. Center on the Developing Child at Harvard University (2009), *Maternal Depression Can Undermine the Development of Young Children: Working Paper No. 8*, https://developingchild.harvard.edu/resources/maternal-depression-can-undermine-the-development-of-young-children/.

2. Newkirk, K., Perry-Jenkins, M., and Sayer, A. G. (2017), "Division of House-hold and Childcare Labor and Relationship Conflict among Low-Income New Parents," *Sex Roles: A Journal of Research*, 5–6, 319, doi:10.1007/s11199-016-0604-3.

3. Lareau, A. (2003), *Unequal Childhoods: Class, Race, and Family Life*, Berkeley: University of California Press.

4. Perry-Jenkins, M., and Wadsworth, S. M. (2017), "Work and Family Research and Theory: Review and Analysis from an Ecological Perspective," *Journal of Family Theory and Review*, 2, 219, doi:10.1111/jftr.12188.

5. Bronfenbrenner, U., and Crouter, A. C. (1982), "Work and Family through Time and Space," in S. B. Kamerman and C. D. Hayes (Eds.), *Families That Work: Children in a Changing World*, 39–83, Washington, DC: National Academy Press.

6. Kohn, M. L., and Schooler, C. (Eds.) (1983), *Work and Personality*, Norwood, NJ: Ablex.

7. Parcel, T. L., and Menaghan, E. G. (1994), *Parents' Jobs and Children's Lives*, New York: Aldine de Gruyter.

8. Barnett, R. C., and Hyde, J. S. (2001), "Women, Men, Work, and Family: An Expansionist Theory," *American Psychologist*, 56 (10), 781–96.

9. Greenberger, E., O'Neil, R., and Nagel, S. K. (1994), "Linking Workplace and Homeplace: Relations between the Nature of Adults' Work and Their Parenting Behaviors," *Developmental Psychology*, 30, 990–1002.

10. Mason, C. A., Cauce, A. M., Gonzales, N., Hiraga, Y., and Grove, K. (1994), "An Ecological Model of Externalizing Behaviors in African-American Adolescents: No Family Is an Island," *Journal of Research on Adolescence*, 4, 639–55.

11. Whitbeck, L. B., Simons, R. L., Conger, R. D., Wickrama, K.A.S., Ackley, K. A., and Elder, G. H., Jr. (1997), "The Effects of Parents' Working Conditions and Family Economic Hardship on Parenting Behaviors and Children's Self-Efficacy," *Social Psychology Quarterly*, 60, 291–303.

12. Costigan, C. L., Cox, M. J., and Cauce, A. M. (2003), "Work-Parenting Linkages among Dual-Earner Couples at the Transition to Parenthood," *Journal of Family Psychology*, 17 (3), 397–408, doi:10.1037/0893-3200.17.3.397.

13. Goodman, W. B., Crouter, A. C., Lanza, S. T., and Cox, M. J. (2008), "Paternal Work Characteristics and Father-Infant Interactions in Low-Income, Rural Families," *Journal of Marriage and Family*, 3, 640.

14. Goodman, W. B., Crouter, A. C., Lanza, S. T., Cox, M. J., and Vernon-Feagans, L. (2011), "Paternal Work Stress and Latent Profiles of Father-Infant Parenting Quality," *Journal of Marriage and Family*, 3, 588.

15. Gassman-Pines, A. (2013), "Daily Spillover of Low-Income Mothers' Perceived Workload to Mood and Mother-Child Interactions," *Journal of Marriage and Family*, 5, 1304.

16. Coley, R. L., and Lombardi, C. M. (2012), "Does Maternal Employment Following Childbirth Support or Inhibit Low-Income Children's Long-Term Development?," *Child Development*, 84 (1) 178–97.

17. Lynd, R. S., and Lynd, H. M. (1929), *Middletown: A Study in Modern American Culture*, New York: Harcourt, Brace, and World.

18. Fathers' reports of work conditions at an earlier time point (four months postpartum) were used to predict the quality of their parenting behavior measured at one year. This lagged timing gives us some faith in the conclusion that work conditions are influencing father behavior, as opposed to the other way around, although to truly discuss causality we need to develop a randomized, intervention study manipulating work conditions.

## Chapter 6. "I Just Want Him to Have a Good Start in Life": Work and Child Development

1. Kohn, M. L. (1977), *Class and Conformity: A Study in Values, with a Reassessment, 1977* (2nd ed.), Chicago: University of Chicago Press.

2. Brooks-Gunn, J., Han, W., and Waldfogel, J. (2010), *First-Year Maternal Employment and Child Development in the First 7 Years*, Monographs of the Society for Research in Child Development, 75 (2).

3. Bowlby, J. (1958), "The Nature of the Child's Tie to His Mother," *International Journal of Psychoanalysis*, 39, 350–73.

4. Brooks-Gunn, Han, and Waldfogel (2010).

5. Lucas-Thompson, R. G., Goldberg, W. A., and Prause, J. (2010), "Maternal Work Early in the Lives of Children and Its Distal Associations with Achievement and Behavior Problems: A Meta-analysis," *Psychological Bulletin*, 136 (6), 915–42, doi:10.1037/a0020875.

6. Coley, R. L., and Lombardi, C. M. (2013), "Does Maternal Employment Following Childbirth Support or Inhibit Low-Income Children's Long-Term Development?," *Child Development*, 84 (1), 178–97, https://doi-org.silk.library.umass.edu/10.1111/j.1467-8624.2012.01840.

7. Dunifon, R., Kalil, A., and Danziger, S. K. (2003), "Maternal Work Behavior under Welfare Reform: How Does the Transition from Welfare to Work Affect Child Development?," *Children and Youth Services Review*, 25 (1–2), 55, https://doi-org.silk.library.umass.edu/10.1016/S0190-7409(02)00266-9.

8. Secret, M., and Peck-Heath, C. (2004), "Maternal Labor Force Participation and Child Well-Being in Public Assistance Families," *Journal of Family Issues*, 25 (4), 520–41.

9. Gerson, K. (2010), *The Unfinished Revolution: How a New Generation Is Reshaping Family, Work and Gender in America*, New York: Oxford University Press.

10. Raley, S., Bianchi, S. M., and Wang, W. (2012), When Do Fathers Care? Mothers' Economic Contribution and Fathers' Involvement in Child Care 1, *American Journal of Sociology*, 5, 1422, doi:10.1086/663354.

11. Family Life Project Key Investigators, Goodman, W. B., Crouter, A. C., Lanza, S. T., Cox, M. J., and Vernon-Feagans L. (2011), "Paternal Work Stress and Latent Profiles of Father-Infant Parenting Quality," *Journal of Marriage and Family*, 73 (3), 588, https://doi-org.silk.library.umass.edu/10.1111/j.1741-3737.2011.00826.x.

12. Parcel, T. L., and Menaghan, E. G. (1994), *Parents' Jobs and Children's Lives*, New York: A. de Gruyter.

13. Yetis-Bayraktar, A., Budig, M. J., and Tomaskovic-Devey, D. (2013), "From the Shop Floor to the Kitchen Floor: Maternal Occupational Complexity and Children's Reading and Math Skills," *Work and Occupations*, 40 (1), 37–64, doi:10.1177/0730888412465879.

14. We tested not only whether autonomy was directly linked to children's social adjustment but whether parenting quality was the conduit linking work conditions to children's outcomes. More details on the analytic approach can be found in Perry-Jenkins, M., Laws, H., Sayer, A., and Newkirk, K. (2019), "Parents' Work and Children's Development: A Longitudinal Investigation of Working-Class Families," *Journal of Family Psychology*, 34 (3), 257–68, https://doi-org.silk.library.umass.edu/10.1037/fam0000580.

## Chapter 7. "Thriving or Surviving": How to Move Forward

1. Vogtman, J., and Schulman, K., 2016, National Women's Law Center, accessed October 31, 2021, https://nwlc.org/resources/set-up-to-fail-when-low-wage-work-jeopardizes-parents-and-childrens-success/.

2. Vogtman and Schulman, 2016.

3. National Public Radio, "House Democrats Pass Bill That Would Protect Worker Organizing Efforts," 2021, accessed October 31, 2021, https://www.npr.org/2021/03/09/975259434/house-democrats-pass-bill-that-would-protect-worker-organizing-efforts.

4. Golden, L., and Wiens-Tuers, B. (2005), "Mandatory Overtime Work in the United States: Who, Where, and What?," *Labor Studies Journal*, 30, 1–26, doi:10.1353/lab.2005.0027.

5. Collins, C. (2019), *Making Motherhood Work: How Women Manage Careers and Caregiving*, Princeton, NJ: Princeton University Press, 261.

6. Kelly, E. L., and Moen, P. (2020), *Overload: How Good Jobs Went Bad and What We Can Do About It*, Princeton, NJ: Princeton University Press, https://workfamilyhealthnetwork.org/about-us.

7. Correll, S. J. (2017), "Reducing Gender Biases in Modern Workplaces: A Small Wins Approach to Organizational Change," SWS 2016 Feminist Lecture, *Gender and Society*, 31 (6), 725–50.

8. Duncan, G. J., and Magnuson, K. (2001), "Off with Hollingshead: Socioeconomic Resources, Parenting and Child Development," in M. Bornstein and R. Bradley (Eds.), *Socioeconomic Status, Parenting and Child Development*, 83–106, Mahwah, NJ: Lawrence Erlbaum.

## Appendixes

1. Perry-Jenkins, M., Repetti, R. L., and Crouter, A. C. (2000), "Work and Family in the 1990s," *Journal of Marriage and Family*, 4, 981.

2. Bronfenbrenner, U. (1979), *The Ecology of Human Development*, Cambridge, MA: Harvard University Press.

3. Bronfenbrenner, U., and Morris, P. A. (2006), "The Bioecological Model of Human Development," in R. M. Lerner and W. Damon (Eds.), *Theoretical Models of Human Development*, 1:793–828, Hoboken, NJ: Wiley and Sons. Also, Bronfenbrenner, U., and Crouter, A. C. (1982), "Work and Family through Time and Space," in S. B. Kamerman and C. D. Hayes (Eds.), *Families That Work: Children in a Changing World*, 39–83, Washington, DC: National Academy Press.

4. Coley, R. L., and Lombardi, C. M. (2013), "Does Maternal Employment Following Childbirth Support or Inhibit Low-Income Children's Long-Term Development?," *Child Development*, 4 (1), 178–97, doi:10.1111/j.1467–8624.2012.01840.x.

5. Lambert, S. J., Haley-Lock, A., and Henly, J. R. (2012), "Schedule Flexibility in Hourly Jobs: Unanticipated Consequences and Promising Directions," *Community, Work and Family*, 15 (3), 293–315, doi:10.1080/13668803.2012.662803.

6. Perry-Jenkins, M., and Folk, K. (1994), "Class, Couples, and Conflict: Effects of the Division of Labor on Assessments of Marriage in Dual-Earner Families," *Journal of Marriage and Family*, 1, 165, doi:10.2307/352711.

7. Bronfenbrenner, U., and Crouter, A. C. (1982).

8. Kohn, M. L. (1977), *Class And Conformity: A Study in Values with a Reassessment, 1977* (2nd ed.), Chicago: University of Chicago Press.

9. Stacy, J., Rogers, T. L., and Menaghan, E. G. (1991), "The Effects of Maternal Working Conditions and Mastery on Child Behavior Problems: Studying the Intergeneration Transmission of Social Control," *Journal of Health and Social Behavior*, 32 (2) 145–64.

10. Meteyer, K. B., and Perry-Jenkins, M. (2009), "Dyadic Parenting and Children's Externalizing Symptoms," *Family Relations*, 58 (3), 289–302.

11. Bolger, N., DeLongis, A., Kessler, R. C., and Wethington, E. (1989), "The Contagion of Stress across Multiple Roles," *Journal of Marriage and Family*, 51 (1), 175–83, https://doi-org.silk.library.umass.edu/10.2307/352378.

12. Glynn, K., Maclean, H., Forte, T., and Cohen, M. (2009), "The Association between Role Overload and Women's Mental Health," *Journal of Women's Health*, 18 (2), 217–23.

13. Keeton Pierce, C., Perry-Jenkins, M., and Sayer, A. (2008), "Sense of Control and Psychological Well-Being during the Transition to Parenthood," *Journal of Family Psychology*, 22 (2), 212–21.

14. Jang, S., Zippay, A., and Park, Rhokeun (2012), "Family Roles as Moderators of the Relationship between Schedule Flexibility and Stress," *Journal of Marriage and Family*, 74 (4), 897–912, https://doi-org.silk.library.umass.edu/10.1111/j.1741-3737 .2012.00984.x.

15. Goodman, W. B., and Crouter, A. C. (2009), "Longitudinal Associations between Maternal Work Stress, Negative Work-Family Spillover and Depressive Symptoms," *Family Relations*, 58 (3), 245–58.

16. Grzywacz, J., Carlons, D., and Shulkin, S. (2008), "Schedule Flexibility and Stress: Linking Formal Flexible Arrangements and Perceived Flexibility to Employee Health," *Community, Work and Family*, 11 (2) 199–214.

17. Brooks-Gunn, J., Han, W. J., and Waldfogel, J. (2010), *First Year Maternal Employment and Child Development in the First 7 Years of Life*, Monographs of the Society for Research in Child Development, 296, 75 (2), New York: Wiley-Blackwell.

18. Roeters, A., Van der Lippe, T., and Kluwer, E. S. (2010), "Work Characteristics and Parent-Child Relationship Quality: The Mediating Role of Temporal Involvement," *Journal of Marriage and Family*, 5, 1317.

19. Walker, L. A., Updegraff, K. A., and Crouter, A. C. (2015), "Mexican-Origin Parents' Work Conditions and Adolescents' Adjustment," *Journal of Family Psychology*, 29 (3), 447–57, https://doi-org.silk.library.umass.edu/10.1037/fam 0000085.

20. Gassman-Pines, A. (2011), "Associations of Low-Income, Working Mothers' Daily Interactions with Supervisors and Mother-Child Interactions," *Journal of Marriage and Family*, 73 (1), 67–76, https://doi-org.silk.library.umass.edu/10.1111/j.1741 -3737.2010.00789.x.

21. National Academy of Sciences, Committee on Occupational Classification and Analysis, "Dictionary of Occupational Titles (DOT): Part I—Current Population Survey, April 1971, Augmented with DOT Characteristics, and Part II—Fourth Edition Dictionary of DOT Scores for 1970 Census Categories" (Computer file), Washington, DC: US Dept. of Commerce, Bureau of the Census (Producer), 197?, Ann Arbor, MI: Inter-university Consortium for Political and Social Research (Distributor), 1981.

22. Parcel, T. L., and Menaghan, E. G. (1994), *Parents' Jobs and Children's Lives*, New York: A. de Gruyter.

23. Raver, C. C. (2003), "Does Work Pay Psychologically as Well as Economically: The Role of Employment in Predicting Depressive Symptoms and Parenting among

Low-Income Families," *Child Development*, 74 (6), 1720–36, https://doi-org.silk .library.umass.edu/10.1046/j.1467-8624.2003.00634.x.

24. Perry-Jenkins, M., Smith, J. Z., Goldberg, A. E., and Logan, J. (2011), "Working-Class Jobs and New Parents' Mental Health," *Journal of Marriage and Family*, 732 (5), 1117–32, https://doi-org.silk.library.umass.edu/10.1111/j.1741-3737.2011.00871.x.

25. Gerson, K. (2010), *The Unfinished Revolution: How a New Generation Is Reshaping Family, Work and Gender in America*, Oxford: Oxford University Press.

26. Goodman, W. B., Crouter, A. C., Lanza, S. T., and Cox, M. J. (2008), "Paternal Work Characteristics and Father-Infant Interactions in Low-Income Rural Families," *Journal of Marriage and Family*, 70 (3), 640–53.

27. Family Life Project Key Investigators, Goodman, W. B., Crouter, A. C., Lanza, S. T., Cox, M. J., and Vernon-Feagans, L. (2011), "Paternal Work Stress and Latent Profiles of Father-Infant Parenting Quality," *Journal of Marriage and Family*, 73 (3), 588–604, https://doi-org.silk.library.umass.edu/10.1111/j.1741-3737.2011.00826.x.

28. Costigan, C. L., Cox, M. J., and Cauce, A. M. (2003), "Work-Parenting Linkages among Dual-Earner Couples at the Transition to Parenthood," *Journal of Family Psychology*, 17 (3), 397–408, https://doi-org.silk.library.umass.edu/10.1037/0893 -3200.17.3.397.

29. Brooks-Gunn, Han, and Waldfogel (2010).

30. Costigan, Cox, and Cauce (2003).

31. Yetis-Bayraktar, A., Budig, M. J., and Tomaskovic-Devey, D. (2013), "From the Shop Floor to the Kitchen Floor: Maternal Occupational Complexity and Children's Reading and Math Skills," *Work and Occupations*, 1, 37.

32. Brooks-Gunn, Han, and Waldfogel (2010).

33. Lucas-Thompson, R. G., Goldberg, W. A., and Prause, J. (2010), "Maternal Work Early in the Lives of Children and Its Distal Associations with Achievement and Behavior Problems: A Meta-analysis," *Psychological Bulletin*, 136 (6), 915, https:// doi-org.silk.library.umass.edu/10.1037/a0020875.

34. Coley and Lombardi (2013).

35. Dunifon, R., Kalil, A., and Danziger, S. K. (2003), "Maternal Work Behavior under Welfare Reform: How Does the Transition from Welfare to Work Affect Child Development?," *Children and Youth Services Review*, 25 (1–2), 55, https://doi-org.silk .library.umass.edu/10.1016/S0190-7409(02)00266-9.

36. Secret, M., and Peck-Heath, C. (2004), "Maternal Labor Force Participation and Child Well-Being in Public Assistance Families," *Journal of Family Issues*, 25 (4), 520–24, https://doi-org.silk.library.umass.edu/10.1177/0192513X03257761.

37. Coley and Lombardi (2013).

38. Lombardi, C. M., and Coley, R. L. (2013), "Low-Income Mothers' Employment Experiences: Prospective Links with Young Children's Development," *Family Relations*, 62 (3), 514–28.

39. Edin, K. J., and Shaefer, H. L. (2015), *$2.00 a Day: Living on Almost Nothing in America*, Boston: Houghton Mifflin Harcourt.

40. Levine, J. A. (2013), *Ain't No Trust: How Bosses, Boyfriends and Bureaucrats Fail Low-Income Mothers and Why It Matters*, Berkeley: University of California Press.

41. Newman, K. S. (2008), *Chutes and Ladders: Navigating the Low-Wage Labor Market*, New York: Russell Sage Foundation at Harvard University Press.

42. Pugh, A. J. (2015), *The Tumbleweed Society: Working and Caring in an Age of Insecurity*, New York: Oxford University Press.

43. Kohn, M. L. (1977), *Class and Conformity: A Study in Values, with a Reassessment, 1977* (2nd ed.), Chicago: University of Chicago Press.

44. Parcel and Menaghan (1994).

45. Yetis-Bayraktar, Budig, and Tomaskovic-Devey, D. (2013), 37.

46. Kohn, M. L., and Schooler, C. (1973), "Occupational Experience and Psychological Functioning: An Assessment of Reciprocal Effects," *American Sociological Review*, 38 (1), 97–118.

47. Parcel and Menaghan (1994).

48. Presser, H. B. (2003), *Working in a 24/7 Economy: Challenges for American Families*, Russell Sage Foundation.

49. Bruce, J., Gunnar, M. R., Pears, K. C., and Fisher, P. A. (2013), "Early Adverse Care, Stress Neurobiology, and Prevention Science: Lessons Learned," *Prevention Science*, 14 (3), 247–56, https://doi-org.silk.library.umass.edu/10.1007/s11121-012-0354-6.

50. Greenberger, E., Goldberg, W. A., Hamill, S. O., O'Neil, R., and Payne, C. (1989), "Contributions of a Supportive Work Environment to Parents' Well-Being and Orientation to Work," *American Journal of Community Psychology*, 17, 755–83, doi:10.1007/BF00922737.

51. Greenberger, E., O'Neil, R., and Nagel, S. K. (1994), "Linking Workplace and Homeplace: Relations between the Nature of Adults' Work and Their Parenting Behaviors," *Developmental Psychology*, 30 (6), 990–1002, doi:10.1037/0012-1649.30.6.990.

52. Greenberger, E., Goldberg, W. A., Hamill, S., O'Neil, R., and Payne, C. (1989), "Contributions of a Supportive Work Environment to Parents' Well-Being and Orientation to Work," *American Journal of Community Psychology*, 17, 755–83.

53. Caplan, R. D., Cobb, S., and French, J. R. (1975), "Relationships of Cessation of Smoking with Job Stress, Personality, and Social Support," *Journal of Applied Psychology*, 60 (2), 211–19.

54. Lambert, S. J., and Hopkins, K. (1995), "Occupational Conditions and Workers' Sense of Community: Variations by Gender and Race," *American Journal of Community Psychology*, 25, 151–79.

55. Perry-Jenkins, M., Seery, B., and Crouter, A. C. (1992), "Linkages between Women's Provider-Role Attitudes, Psychological Well-Being, and Family Relationships," *Psychology of Women Quarterly*, 16 (3): 311–29, doi:10.1111/j.1471–6402.1992.tb00257.x.

56. Spence, J. T. (1973), "The Attitudes toward Women Scale: An Objective Instrument to Measure Attitudes toward the Rights and Roles of Women in Contemporary Society," *American Psychological Association*, https://search-ebscohost-com.silk.library.umass.edu/login.aspx?direct=true&db=cat06087a&AN=umass.001783085&site=eds-live&scope=site.

57. Brogan, D., and Kutner, N. G. (1973), "Measuring Sex-Role Orientation: A Normative Approach," *Journal of Marriage and the Family*, 38:31–40.

58. McCrae, R. R., and Costa, P. T. (1987), "Validation of the Five-Factor Model of Personality across Instruments and Observers," *Journal of Personality and Social Psychology*, 52 (1), 81–90, https://doi.org/10.1037/0022-3514.52.1.81.

59. Radloff, L. S. (1977), "The CES-D Scale: A Self-Report Depression Scale for Research in the General Population," *Applied Psychological Measurement*, 1 (3), 385–401, doi:10.1177/014662167700100306.

60. Spielberger, C. D. (1972), *Anxiety: Current Trends, Theories and Research*, vol. 1. New York: Academic.

61. Reilly, M. D. (1982), "Working Wives and Consumption," *Journal of Consumer Research*, 8, 407–18.

62. Rosenberg, M. (1979), *Conceiving the Self*, New York: Basic Books.

63. Ross, C. E. (1991), "Marriage and the Sense of Control," *Journal of Marriage and the Family*, 53, 831–38.

64. Cox, J. L., Holden, J. M., and Sagovsky, R. (1987), "Detection of Postnatal Depression: Development of the 10-Item Edinburgh Postnatal Depression Scale," *British Journal of Psychiatry*, 150:782–86.

65. Skinner, D. A., and McCubbin, H. I. (1991), "The Dual-Employed Coping Scales," in H. I. McCubbin and M. A. Thompson (Eds.), *Family Assessment Inventories for Research and Practice*, 265–78, Madison: University of Wisconsin Press.

66. Braiker, H. B., and Kelley, H. H. (1979), "Conflict in the Development of Close Relationships," in R. L. Burgess and T. L. Huston (Eds.), *Social Exchange in Developing Relationships*, 135–68, New York: Academic.

67. Kurdek, L. A. (1994), "Conflict Resolution Styles in Gay, Lesbian, Heterosexual Nonparent, and Heterosexual Parent Couples," *Journal of Marriage and Family* 56 (3), 705–22, doi:10.2307/352880.

68. Pierce, G. R., Sarason, I. G., and Sarason, B. R. (1991), "General and Relationship-Based Perceptions of Social Support: Are Two Constructs Better Than One?," *Journal of Personality and Social Psychology*, 61 (6), 1028–39, https://doi-org.silk.library.umass.edu/10.1037/0022-3514.61.6.1028.

69. Barnett, R. C., and Baruch, G. K. (1987), "Determinants of Fathers' Participation in Family Work," *Journal of Marriage and the Family*, 49 (1), 29–40, doi:10.2307/352667.

70. Barnett and Baruch (1987).

71. Barnett and Baruch (1987) (modified).

72. Procidano, M. E., and Heller, K. (1983), "Measures of Perceived Social Support from Friends and from Family: Three Validation Studies," *American Journal of Community Psychology*, 11 (1), 1–24, https://doi.org/10.1007/BF00898416.

73. Procidano and Heller (1983).

74. Fiala, W., Bjorck, J., and Goruch, R. (2002), "The Religious Support Scale: Construction, Validation and Cross-Validation," *American Journal of Community Psychology*, 30, 761–86.

75. McNeilly, M. D., Anderson, N. B., Robinson, E. L., McManus, C. H., Armstead, C. A., Clark, R., Pieper, C. F., Simons, C., and Saulter, T. D. (1996), "Convergent, Discriminant and Concurrent Validity of the Perceived Racism Scale: A Multidimensional Assessment of the Experience of White Racism among African Americans," in R. L. Jones (Ed.), *Handbook of Tests and Measurements for Black Populations*, 359–74, Richmond, CA: Cobb and Henry.

76. Phinney, J. (1992), "The Multigroup Ethnic Identity Measure: A New Scale for Use with Adolescents and Young Adults from Diverse Groups," *Journal of Adolescent Research*, 7, 156–76.

77. Fiese, B. H., and Kline, C. A. (1993), "Development of the Family Ritual Questionnaire: Initial Reliability and Validation Studies," *Journal of Family Psychology*, 6 (3), 290–99, https://doi.org/10.1037/0893-3200.6.3.290.

78. Shelton, K. K., Frick, P. J., and Wootton, J. (1996), "Assessment of Parenting Practices in Families of Elementary School-Age Children," *Journal of Clinical Child Psychology*, 25 (September): 317–29, https://search-ebscohost-com.silk.library.umass.edu/login.aspx?direct=true&db=ssa&AN=512842881&site=eds-live&scope=site.

79. Arnold, D. S., O'Leary, S. G., Wolff, L. S., and Acker, M. M. (1993), "The Parenting Scale: A Measure of Dysfunctional Parenting in Discipline Situations," *Psychological Assessment*, 5, 137–44.

80. Abidin, R. R. (1997), "Parenting Stress Index: A Measure of the Parent-Child System," in C. P. Zalaquett and R. J. Wood (Eds.), *Evaluating Stress: A Book of Resources*, 277–91, Lanham, MD: Scarecrow Education.

81. Arnold, O'Leary, Wolff, and Acker (1993).

82. Shelton, Frick, and Wootton. (1996).

83. Newland, R. P., Crnic, K. A., Cox, M. J., and Mills-Koonce, W. R. (2013), "The Family Model Stress and Maternal Psychological Symptoms: Mediated Pathways from Economic Hardship to Parenting," *Journal of Family Psychology* 27 (1), 96–105, doi:10.1037/a0031112.

84. National Institute of Child Health and Human Development Early Child Care Research Network (1999), "Chronicity of Maternal Depressive Symptoms, Maternal Sensitivity, and Child Functioning at 36 Months," *Developmental Psychology*, 35, 1297–310, doi:10.1037/0012–1649.35.5.1297.

85. Braun, V., and Clarke, V. (2006), "Using Thematic Analysis in Psychology," *Qualitative Research in Psychology*, 3, 77–101, https://doi-org.silk.library.umass.edu /10.1191/1478088.

# INDEX

A page number in *italics* refers to a figure.